INTERNATIONAL AND REGIONAL

Headwinds threaten nascent recovery

- The outlook for the global economy has deteriorated significantly. The Russian invasion of Ukraine has contributed to surging commodity prices and disruptions in trade and financial linkages. In Asia and the Pacific, higher prices for fuel and food will have an adverse effect on consumers and lead to widening fiscal deficits. Rising inflation has spurred the withdrawal of monetary stimulus, and the risk of an inflationary spiral may prompt even more aggressive tightening. Meanwhile, the coronavirus disease (COVID-19) pandemic has eroded fiscal policy space, leaving many economies with limited ability to respond to the latest crisis. Moreover, lockdowns in key cities in the People's Republic of China (PRC) have weighed on global economic activity and supply chains. Global growth is projected to slow to 3.6% in 2022 and 2023. Downside risks include a worsening of the invasion, escalation of sanctions, a sharper slowdown in the PRC, and renewed COVID-19 outbreaks and the emergence of more virulent strains. Developing Asia is expected to grow by 4.6% in 2022 and 5.2% in 2023.

- The Pacific is expected to return to growth in 2022 and 2023. The subregion is expected to grow by 4.7% this year and 5.4% next year as most economies emerge from the worst of the pandemic-induced downturn. Nonetheless, substantial risks persist: many countries continue to experience community transmission of COVID-19 as vaccination coverage remains low in others. On the external front, the surge in international prices could stoke inflation, erode purchasing power, and increase trade and fiscal deficits. Also, faster-than-expected monetary policy normalization in advanced economies may dampen global demand and fuel financial market volatility. However, in Papua New Guinea, higher commodity prices are expected to benefit the recovery in the minerals sector. High visitor arrivals are expected to support tourism-dependent economies such as Fiji, the Cook Islands, and Palau. Meanwhile, contractions are expected this year in Tonga because of a major volcanic eruption in January, and in Samoa and Solomon Islands due to mobility restrictions in response to local outbreaks of COVID-19 in the first quarter.

- The United States economy contracted by 1.5% in the first quarter of 2022 because of an outbreak of the Omicron variant of COVID-19. Private consumption grew by 3.1%, but weak investment and declines in government spending and net exports weighed on gross domestic product (GDP) growth. For the rest of the year, consumer spending is expected to remain strong, and investments should recover as inventory levels normalize. Government spending will be limited by the withdrawal of fiscal stimulus, and net exports will stay negative because of rising import costs. Full-year economic growth is forecast at 2.2% moderating to 1.7% in 2023 with considerable uncertainty. The main downside risk relates to surging inflation caused by supply-chain disruptions and the impact of the Russian invasion of Ukraine. Consequently, uncertainty surrounds the pace of monetary tightening that is needed to rein in inflation. Steep interest rate hikes and faster-than-expected unwinding of monetary support raise concerns of a possible recession and financial market volatility.

- Economic growth in the PRC moderated to 4.8% in the first quarter and further to 0.4% in the second quarter of 2022. Sporadic COVID-19 outbreaks led to lockdowns and mobility restrictions in April in key cities, notably Shanghai and Beijing. Marked slowdowns were seen in manufacturing, infrastructure, and property investment though preliminary indicators showed signs of improvement starting in May. Nevertheless, economic disruption and rising inflation have negatively affected household consumption while the real estate industry, a key economic sector, remains weak. GDP growth is forecast at 4.0% in 2022 and 4.8% in 2023.

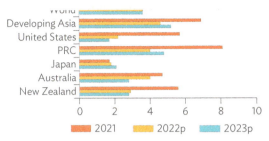

ADB = Asian Development Bank, GDP = gross domestic product, p = projection, PRC = People's Republic of China.

Notes: Developing Asia as defined by ADB. Figures are based on ADB estimates except for Australia, New Zealand, and world.

Sources: ADB. *Asian Development Outlook (ADO) Series*. FocusEconomics. 2022. FocusEconomics Consensus Forecast Australia & New Zealand June 2022. Barcelona; and International Monetary Fund. 2022. *World Economic Outlook: War sets back the global recovery*. Washington, DC (April).

GDP Growth in Developing Asia (%, annual)

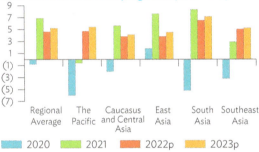

( ) = negative, GDP = gross domestic product, p = projection.
Source: ADB. *Asian Development Outlook (ADO) Series*.

COVID-19 Vaccination Coverage in the Pacific (% of total population)

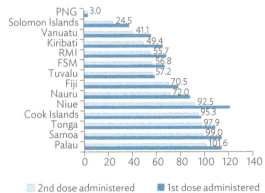

COVID-19 = coronavirus disease, FSM = Federated States of Micronesia, PNG = Papua New Guinea, RMI = Republic of the Marshall Islands.

Note: Data as of 15 July 2022.

Sources: Pacific Data Hub. COVID-19 vaccination (accessed 15 July 2022); and authors' calculations.

COVID-19 Cases in the Pacific

	Total Cases	Active Cases	Total Deaths	Total Cases /1,000 Population
Fiji	66,713	1,524	869	73.34
PNG	44,758	114	662	4.82
Solomon Islands	21,544	5,034	153	29.88
Samoa	15,134	13,500	29	75.26
Tonga	12,382	147	12	114.51
Vanuatu	11,690	174	14	36.34
Nauru	6,930	3,758	1	632.18
Cook Islands	5,827	24	1	331.14
Palau	5,308	255	6	290.55
Kiribati	3,236	558	13	26.27
RMI	47	29	–	0.78
FSM	38	5	–	0.32
Niue	26	3	–	15.78
Tuvalu	3	3	–	0.25
World	565,166,682	22,005,691	6,381,885	72.51

– = none, COVID-19 = coronavirus disease, FSM = Federated States of Micronesia, PNG = Papua New Guinea, RMI = Republic of the Marshall Islands.

Note: Data as of 15 July 2022.

Sources: Worldometer. *Worldometer COVID-19 Data and Population* (accessed 15 July 2022); and authors' calculations.

- A surge in COVID-19 cases driven by the Omicron variant weighed on the Japanese economy in the first quarter of 2022. GDP declined by 0.5% on an annualized basis during the quarter. Private consumption has remained strong but is facing increasing pressure in the short-term from rising consumer prices exacerbated by the impact of the Russian invasion of Ukraine on commodity prices, supply disruptions, and a depreciating yen. Weaker net exports owing to the impact of lockdowns in the PRC on manufacturing supply chains underpin a GDP growth forecast of 1.8% in 2022, picking up to 2.1% in 2023. Further relaxation of entry requirements for international tourists will aid economic growth and help support the yen.

- Australia's economy expanded 0.8% in the first quarter of 2022. This is the second consecutive quarter that its seasonally adjusted GDP grew since the contraction in the third quarter of 2021 because of the Delta outbreak. Strong domestic demand prevailed over weather events, with household spending increasing by 1.5% as spending on discretionary goods grew higher than pre-COVID-19 pandemic levels for the first time. The reopening of international and domestic borders supported growth in transport services, recreation and culture, and hotels and restaurants. Government spending on health and disaster response to regions affected by recent weather events translated into a 2.7% increase in the first quarter. Economic growth remains robust as the new government takes over the helm. FocusEconomics expects full-year growth to be at 4.0% in 2022 and 2.8% in 2023.

- Economic activity in New Zealand fell 0.2% in the first quarter of 2022. After growing in the fourth quarter of 2021, the seasonally adjusted GDP contracted in the next quarter as the Omicron variant outbreak weakened output across key industries. Primary industries' production dropped 1.2% with mining contracting by 8.9% and agriculture and fisheries falling by 4.8%. There was lower output as well in the goods-producing industries, which declined by 0.1%, mainly driven by the 1.4% contraction in manufacturing. On the expenditure side of the GDP, these developments translated into lower exports which decreased by 14.3%. Despite this, growth prospects remain optimistic as the gradual lifting of restrictions is expected to boost tourism. Higher interest rates and energy prices though pose downside risks. FocusEconomics forecasts a growth of 2.9% in 2022 and 2.8% in 2023.

Prices soar as the Russian invasion of Ukraine disrupts global supply channels

- The invasion led to the disruption of the Russian Federation's export of crude oil, which accounts for 10% of global oil production. The price of Brent crude oil jumped 63% in the first quarter of 2022 (year-on-year) as global supply contracted because of import bans on Russian oil imposed by several countries. Global consumption of crude oil has fallen since the start of 2022 partly because of this but also because of subdued global economic activity and COVID-19 outbreaks in the PRC. Crude oil price is expected to remain at about $100 per barrel in 2022, a 42% increase compared to the previous year. This is projected to fall by about 8% in 2023.

- Agricultural commodity prices surged in the first quarter of 2022. The World Bank's food price index increased by almost 25% (year-on-year) amid trade and production disruptions because of the Russian invasion of Ukraine. The surge in prices was also driven by higher input costs and recovering animal feed demand, particularly in the PRC. With Ukraine accounting for 10% of global exports of wheat and almost 4% of global maize production, the closure of Ukrainian ports has significantly reduced global grain supply. Ukraine is also the world's major producer of sunflower oil and the barriers to exports, together with Indonesia's ban on exports of palm oil, have contributed to the higher food price index. The full-year forecast expects the food price index to rise by 23% in 2022 before moderating in 2023. Prolonged war in Ukraine, weather events, and macroeconomic uncertainties pose risks to the forecast.

Average Spot Price of Brent Crude Oil
(monthly, $/barrel)

Source: World Bank. 2022. *World Bank Commodity Price Data (Pink Sheet)*.

Food Prices
(2018 = 100, annual)

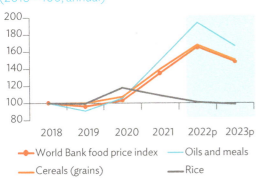

p = projection.
Sources: ADB calculations using data from World Bank. 2022. *Commodity Markets Outlook: The Impact of War in Ukraine on Commodity Markets, April 2022.* Washington, DC; and World Bank. *World Bank Commodity Price Data* (Pink Sheet) (accessed 17 June 2022).

Prices of Export Commodities
(2018 = 100, annual)

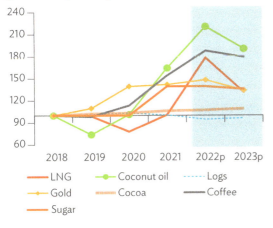

LNG = liquefied natural gas, p = projection.
Sources: ADB calculations using data from World Bank. 2022. *Commodity Markets Outlook: The Impact of War in Ukraine on Commodity Markets, April 2022.* Washington, DC; and World Bank. *World Bank Commodity Price Data* (Pink Sheet) (accessed 17 June 2022).

Tourist Departures Bound for Pacific Destinations
('000 persons, January–April totals)

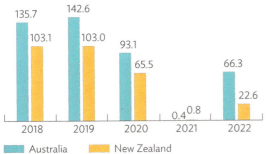

Sources: Australian Bureau of Statistics and Statistics New Zealand.

Lead authors: Noel Del Castillo, Remrick Patagan, and Rommel Rabanal.

- Steep increases in natural gas prices because of the ongoing invasion in Ukraine were also reflected in the liquefied natural gas price as it rose 67% in the first quarter of 2022. Despite higher production of liquefied natural gas, stronger demand for the commodity is expected to push the price higher in the succeeding quarters this year, with the full-year forecast indicating a 77% growth in prices for 2022 before falling by 26% in 2023. Gold prices likewise advanced by 4% in the first quarter of 2022, buoyed by rising inflation and heightened geopolitical risks. While the full-year price growth of gold for 2022 is expected to mimic its first quarter performance, it is projected to fall by almost 10% in 2023 as major economies implement tighter monetary policies. While prices of coconut oil and coffee are projected to increase sharply in 2022, other Pacific export commodities such as cocoa and sugar are expected to remain flat. Log prices are seen to fall by 6% in 2022 before rising 2% in 2023.

Green shoots in tourism to the Pacific

- Following an extended pause in international tourism since April 2020, visitor arrivals in some Pacific destinations have resumed as of early 2022. Progress in national vaccination programs has allowed for reopening to fully vaccinated tourists while minimizing health risks.

- In the South Pacific, Fiji officially reopened its borders to international tourists in December 2021, resulting in a sharp rise in arrivals—particularly from the main markets of Australia and New Zealand. During January–April 2022, the number of Australian tourists bound for Fiji reached almost 66,000, or about two-thirds of the pre-pandemic level for the same period. Tourism to Fiji from New Zealand was more modest at about 6,600 and remained at only 15% of the pre-pandemic numbers. For the Cook Islands, the resumption of quarantine-free travel with New Zealand in January 2022 saw the number of tourists from that primary market reach a total of almost 15,000 over the first 4 months of the year. This is equivalent to about 62% of pre-pandemic arrivals during the same period. By contrast, Samoa and Tonga have remained closed to international tourists. Vanuatu reopened its borders in July 2022 with flights from Australia and New Zealand.

- Palau implemented a travel bubble with Taipei,China in April 2021. This has operated intermittently as outbreaks in both Taipei,China (in May 2021) and Palau (in January 2022) have led to suspensions of the arrangement. Palau also reopened its borders to fully vaccinated tourists in mid-2021 via flights through Guam. These measures enabled steady gains in tourist arrivals, which recovered slightly to more than 4,600 (about 10% of pre-pandemic levels) during the second half of 2021. Despite an Omicron outbreak in January 2022, the number of tourists in the first quarter of 2022 held at more than 1,500 or 6% of pre-pandemic arrivals. The restoration of direct flight links with the Philippines in April 2022, and potentially with Japan and the Republic of Korea later in the year as these markets likewise reopen to international tourism, provide some optimism for increased arrivals for the rest of the year.

SPECIAL FEATURE

The Impacts of the Russian Invasion of Ukraine on the Pacific

The Russian invasion of Ukraine is seen to have relatively little direct impact on ADB's Pacific developing member countries (DMCs), given limited economic linkages with both countries and the wider European region. However, indirect impacts—through commodity prices, global growth prospects affecting major economic partners, and exchange rate movements—are seen to be more significant. This special feature examines the channels through which the war would impact Pacific economies, estimates the possible extent of these impacts, and explores the various mitigating measures implemented by governments.

DIRECT IMPACTS

Minimal trade impact is expected, given low dependence on the European/Russian markets, but with some upside risk for Papua New Guinea (PNG). Europe is a relatively small trading partner for the Pacific. The two largest partners are Solomon Islands and PNG, which ship about 15% and less than 10% of their exports, respectively, to the region. Trade with the Russian Federation is less than 1% for both economies. These exports may be affected if the war escalates, but PNG may also benefit from potential increases in export opportunities, particularly for minerals and hydrocarbons that comprise more than 80% of its export basket.

Distance likewise translates to weak tourism linkages between the Pacific and Europe/Russian Federation. European visitors to the Cook Islands, Fiji, Palau, Samoa, and Vanuatu averaged 5.7% of total arrivals in recent years. (No similar data for Tonga are available, but more than 85% of its total visitors come from neighboring countries and the United States [US].) Russian visitors averaged 0.2% of total arrivals to the Cook Islands and Fiji, the only two Pacific DMCs that track arrivals from this source market.

The Russian invasion of Ukraine is seen also to have a limited impact on Pacific DMCs' external financing in the near term. External financing in the subregion comes mostly in the form of remittances and grants from development partners, while some of the larger economies can attract foreign direct investment. Key sources of remittances are Australia, New Zealand, and the US. Development support has mostly come from the World Bank, ADB, and United Nations-attached agencies; and bilateral partners Australia, Japan, New Zealand, the People's Republic of China, Taipei,China, and the US, though some Pacific DMCs are expecting grant support from the European Union in the next 2–3 years. There is minimal exposure to international capital markets and foreign investors, with most countries having small financial sectors. For the smaller economies, the impact of the war may be felt through volatility in the investment income of their sovereign trust funds.

INDIRECT IMPACTS

The Pacific's remoteness compounds the impacts of commodity price shocks. For most Pacific DMCs, fuel represents a large share of total imports, although these come mostly from Asia, Australia, New Zealand, and the US. Imported fuel accounts for a substantial share of total imports across the subregion, ranging from 6.7% in the Marshall Islands, 13.0% in Kiribati, 14.4% in the Cook Islands, 14.6% in Samoa, 20.0 % in Tuvalu, 22.0% in Fiji, and 58.2% in Nauru. Only PNG is an exporter of petroleum products, i.e., crude oil and liquefied natural gas, and stands to benefit from higher international prices.

Given the Pacific's import dependence and extreme remoteness, relative to even its small island developing states peers in the Caribbean, international fuel price shocks generally translate into compounding impacts across most commodities. Based on the observed sensitivity of consumer prices across the subregion to oil price movements during the particularly volatile period covering 2007–2011, the potential additional inflationary impact of the recent oil price shock because of the Russian invasion of Ukraine can be gauged to average about 1.6 percentage points across the Pacific DMCs, with larger impacts for smaller and more remote DMCs, particularly the Marshall Islands and Nauru (Figure 1).

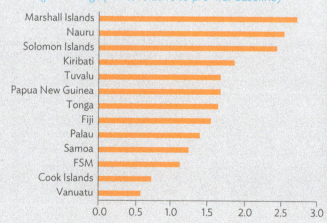

Figure 1: Potential Increases in 2022 Inflation Due to Oil Price Hikes Since the Russian Invasion of Ukraine
(percentage points relative to pre-war baseline)

FSM = Federated States of Micronesia.
Note: The graph compares the projected inflation rates based on a crude oil price projection for 2022 of $109 per barrel, relative to inflation projections under a baseline price of $74 per barrel that prevailed prior to the Russian invasion of Ukraine in late February.
Sources: ADB estimates using data from the Asian Development Outlook and Pacific Economic Monitor databases.

Further, elevated crude oil and international transport prices can translate also into expanding import bills. During 2009–2010, when crude oil prices rose at a rate of only about half the projected increase in 2022, import bill expansion as a percentage of gross domestic product already reached double digits in the Marshall Islands, Solomon Islands, Niue, and Tuvalu (Table). Given that the magnitude of the projected crude oil price spike for 2022 is about 1.9 times the increase recorded in 2009–2010, import bill expansion as a percentage of gross domestic product during this current period of elevated prices could again potentially reach double digits in those economies along with Fiji, PNG, and Samoa.

It is worth noting that countries that have moved faster in transitioning to renewable energy sources stand to benefit from a more muted inflationary impact of imported fuel. Countries with the lowest shares of renewables to total energy production such as the Marshall Islands (2%), Nauru (2%), and Solomon Islands (6%) are projected to see larger increases in consumer prices from rising oil prices. This provides further impetus for these countries to accelerate the shift toward renewable energy. ADB continues to support the renewable energy transition in the Pacific through improvements to renewable energy generation and infrastructure in Tonga; construction of a hydropower plant in Vanuatu to help replace existing diesel generation; and installation of a solar photovoltaic and battery energy storage system in Kiribati.

Recent developments point to surging inflation. Although some controls have been set to mitigate impacts on consumers, there are already indications of significant price increases in staple food items, e.g., eggs, fish, and canned goods, in the Pacific. In Fiji, price increases have been observed in breads and pastries, given higher prices for wheat and other imported inputs largely because of the Russian invasion of Ukraine. Besides household budgets, these developments could have serious implications on hospital food services and school feeding programs.

Further, marked increases in retail fuel prices have been observed in most Pacific DMCs since March. In Majuro, the capital of the Marshall Islands, fuel prices are reported to have increased by more than 40% over the past 15 months, breaching the $7 per gallon mark in April. In more remote parts of the Marshall Islands, fuel reportedly costs about $10 per gallon (Johnson 2022). (Retail fuel price trends are explored in more detail on page 10.) In Tonga, the higher price of diesel that took effect in mid-March led to the Electricity Commission approving a 7.6% hike in electricity tariffs (Matangi Tonga 2022a).

Bus drivers in Vanuatu have requested the government to increase fares, and bus fares in Fiji were raised by more than a third partly to cushion the impact of rising fuel prices (Pratap 2022). In Solomon Islands, the index for transport rose 12.8% (year-on-year) to April 2022, while the index for food was up 7.5% and housing utilities (electricity, water, and gas) rose by 5.4%.

Table: Impact of Most Recent Oil Price Shock on Trade Balance
(illustrative figures based on 2009–2010 experience to gauge possible 2022 impacts)

Pacific DMC	Change in Import Bill		Change in Trade Balance	
	($ million)	(% of 2009 GDP)	($ million)	(% of 2009 GDP)
Cook Islands	0.6	0.3	15.8	7.9
Fiji	203.9	6.6	(28.8)	(0.9)
Kiribati	5.7	4.3	(6.4)	(4.8)
Marshall Islands	32.8	21.8	(16.9)	(11.2)
Micronesia, Federated States of	6.6	2.4	(1.4)	(0.5)
Nauru	...	...	...	...
Niue	1.8	12.9	(2.0)	(13.9)
Palau	8.4	4.6	(5.4)	(2.9)
Papua New Guinea	661.1	5.7	696.6	6.0
Samoa	36.4	6.8	(29.5)	(5.6)
Solomon Islands	121.3	15.0	(62.3)	(7.7)
Tonga	(24.0)	(7.6)	24.4	7.7
Tuvalu	2.9	10.0	6.7	23.3
Vanuatu	(4.2)	(0.7)	0.1	0.0

... = data not available, ( ) = negative, DMC = developing member country, GDP = gross domestic product.
Notes: Figures are derived from actual data from 2009 to 2010, when Brent crude oil prices increased by 28.7% (from $61.90 per barrel to $79.60), which is only about half of the projected 54.7% rise projected from $70.40 per barrel in 2021 to a with-conflict forecast of $109.00 for 2022. The forecast is based on the average futures path from 24 May to 6 June 2022, driven by a prolonged Russian invasion of Ukraine, supply constraints, and post-coronavirus disease economic recovery. Oil prices are expected to fall in the third quarter but will remain highly volatile due to low global inventories.
Sources: ADB estimates using data from the Asian Development Outlook and Pacific Economic Monitor databases.

Besides food and retail fuel costs, higher fuel prices also have pushed up the landed costs of imported goods because of their impact on transport. Concerns have been raised in the Marshall Islands about the prospective spike in the prices of construction materials, all of which must be imported. Besides private construction, this will affect public investment projects such as a planned hospital upgrade.

In May, inflation in Samoa was estimated at 8.9%, driven by double-digit price growth in clothing, transport, food, and communication. In Palau, consumer price inflation spiked to 10.6% (year-on-year) during the March quarter of 2022 on increases in cost of utilities, transport, and food inflation. This reflects both direct impacts of elevated fuel prices and the pass-through effect of higher transport costs for imported commodities.

The Russian invasion of Ukraine could further depress global sentiment and global growth prospects. Increased risk aversion leading to a decline in global business and consumer sentiment could affect Pacific DMCs, particularly larger, more trade-oriented economies. A corresponding flight to safety could also cause tighter global financial conditions, constraining foreign investment and capital spending.

Meanwhile, a weaker external environment, along with higher energy prices, could dampen demand for goods and services exports from key trading partners such as Australia, New Zealand, the PRC, and the US. This would include fewer visitor arrivals from these countries, most of whom are also the main source markets for the subregion's tourism-dependent economies, as escalating transport costs (along with health concerns and travel disincentives related to the ongoing coronavirus disease [COVID-19] pandemic) keep would-be visitors at home and increases the likelihood of long-term economic scarring, especially in the tourism sector.

Diverse currency regimes among Pacific DMCs indicate differential impacts on regional exchange rates. All Pacific DMCs are heavily import-dependent which makes them vulnerable to exchange rate-induced inflation.

- For the North Pacific economies that rely on the US dollar ($),[1] faster-than-expected monetary tightening and capital flight to the US is driving US dollar appreciation which may mitigate imported inflation.
- Countries that use the Australian (A$)[2] and New Zealand dollar (NZ$)[3] face depreciation pressures if the US dollar continues to strengthen. Higher commodity prices could benefit the Australian dollar via energy and mineral exports and disadvantage the New Zealand dollar via increased input costs of its agricultural exports, but further deterioration in the external environment could dampen broader demand for exports.
- Among countries that have their own currencies,[4] PNG also stands to benefit from higher energy and mineral prices, but a downturn in global sentiment could also exacerbate its persistently negative capital account through lower foreign direct investment. Nevertheless, the kina is expected to be stable.

- Other DMCs with their own currencies utilize exchange rate pegs to baskets of currencies from their major trading partners, mostly the Australian dollar, the New Zealand dollar, and the US dollar. Movements in these currencies generally track those of the Australian dollar and the New Zealand dollar, and will largely depend on developments in the Australian and New Zealand economies outlined above.

The inflationary impact of the war has accelerated the withdrawal of monetary stimulus, leading to higher global interest rates and tighter financial conditions. To a certain extent, Pacific DMCs are insulated from increased financing costs due to their relatively limited access to international capital markets and reliance on grants and concessional loans from their development partners. In the longer run, however, rising global interest rates could eventually filter into financing costs of development partners and potentially affect even concessional lending facilities.

CONCLUSION AND RECOMMENDATIONS

Although the Russian invasion of Ukraine is seen to have minimal direct impacts due to Pacific economies' limited ties to these countries and Europe as a whole, it would have significant indirect impacts as these remote, highly import-dependent economies must deal with escalating international commodity prices, especially for fuel, and a dampened global economic outlook.

Higher prices of staple foods, retail pump prices, and transport costs have reached consumers and many Pacific governments have unveiled public relief measures in response to these rising price pressures. These include tax exemptions and waiver of import duties on selected key commodity items such as staple foods and fuel (Fiji, PNG, Solomon Islands); and subsidies for the cost of public utilities, notably electricity, as well as for fuel (Nauru, PNG, Solomon Islands, Tonga). Other countries have generally increased government spending and are pursuing expansionary fiscal policy (the Cook Islands); or are increasing government borrowing requirements (Samoa) or passing supplementary budgets (Vanuatu). There are also direct income support measures in the form of wage and pension adjustments (the Cook Islands) and ex-gratia payments for public employees to ease higher living costs (Nauru).

Many Pacific DMCs have forgone monetary independence and are thus reliant on fiscal policy to respond to the current inflationary shock. An expansionary fiscal policy, however, risks contributing to inflation and should be targeted toward the sectors most in need of assistance. Moreover, there is considerable uncertainty on the duration and intensity of current price pressures which would depend on various factors such as whether the war becomes protracted or even turn into a "frozen conflict,"[5] the ability of central banks to prevent an inflationary spiral, and the path of the post-COVID-19 recovery. A prudent approach, through targeted and quality spending, would preserve much-needed fiscal space and allow governments to retain enough resources to respond to a worsening of current conditions and any future contingencies.

Lead authors: Prince Cruz, Noel Del Castillo, Remrick Patagan, Rommel Rabanal, and Cara Tinio.

Endnotes

1. The Federated States of Micronesia, the Marshall Islands, and Palau.
2. Kiribati, Nauru, and Tuvalu.
3. The Cook Islands and Niue.
4. Fiji, Papua New Guinea, Samoa, Solomon Islands, Tonga, and Vanuatu.
5. In international diplomacy, the term generally refers to unresolved disputes affecting countries of the Black Sea region (Tisdall 2010). A cessation of war in Ukraine without a political solution could lead to an indefinite suspension of Ukranian commodity exports via the Black Sea and continued economic sanctions on the Russian Federation.

References

Bank of Papua New Guinea. *Quarterly Economic Bulletin Statistical Tables* (accessed March 2022).

Central Bank of Samoa. *Visitor earnings & remittances* (accessed March 2022).

Fiji Bureau of Statistics. *Visitor Arrivals Statistics* (accessed March 2022).

Government of the Cook Islands, Ministry of Finance and Economic Management. *Tourism and Migration Statistics* (accessed March 2022).

Government of the Cook Islands, Ministry of Finance and Economic Management. 2022. *Cook Islands Government Budget Estimates 2022/23*. Rarotonga.

Government of Samoa. 2022. *Fiscal Strategy Statement 2022/2023*. Apia.

The Island Sun. 2022a. Hike in Fuel Price Affects Fishermen. 11 May.

The Island Sun. 2022b. Government: Fuel Prices Down by $0.35 per Litre. 2 June.

Johnson, G. 2022. *Skyrocketing prices hit Marshall Islands*. Radio New Zealand. 17 May.

Kumar, K. 2022. *Government to ensure stability*. Fiji Broadcasting Corporation News. 14 June.

Matangi Tonga. 2022. Electricity Tariff increase from 1 April 2022. 4 April.

Nand, E. 2022. *Increase in non price-controlled bread products*. Fiji Broadcasting Corporation News. 23 March.

National Reserve Bank of Tonga. 2022. *Monthly Economic Review for March 2022*. 13 June.

Pratap, R. 2022. *FBOA welcomes fare increase*. Fiji Broadcasting Corporation News. 7 May.

Reserve Bank of Vanuatu. 2021. *Quarterly Economic Review September 2021*. Port Vila.

Samoa Bureau of Statistics. 2022. *Consumer Price Index May 2022*. Apia.

The Secretariat of the Pacific Regional Environment Programme. 2020. *State of the environment and conservation in the Pacific Islands: 2020 regional report.*

Solomon Islands National Statistics Office. 2022. *National Consumer Price Index (April 2022)*. Honiara.

Tisdall, S. 2010. The Dangerous New World of Self-Interested Nations. *The Guardian*. 22 September.

United Nations. *Comtrade Database* (accessed March 2022).

Vanuatu Daily Post. 2022. Bus Drivers Demand Fare Increase. 23 April.

Retail Fuel Prices in the Pacific, March–June 2022

The Russian invasion of Ukraine has had a significant impact on commodity prices, spurring higher consumer prices globally. The Pacific has been particularly affected by increases in fuel prices. In the second quarter of 2022, prices of fuel in Micronesia rose by an average of 2.3% a month relative to March 2022 (Figure 2), while the increases in Melanesia averaged 9.4% a month (Figure 3). The highest increases, averaging 12.5% a month, occurred in Polynesia (Figure 4). Trends have varied because of measures that were affecting costs, such as taxes and subsidies, and because some Pacific economies were using up previously imported fuel stocks.

Lead authors: Remrick Patagan and Cara Tinio.

Thank you to ADB Pacific Country Office, Resident Mission, and Regional Office colleagues for tracking retail fuel prices for the *Pacific Economic Monitor*:

Cook Islands: Lavinia Tama and Amber Raymond

Fiji: Isoa Wainiqolo

Kiribati: Teatao Tira

Federated States of Micronesia: Maybelline Andon-Bing and Alan Semens

Marshall Islands: Ellen Paul and Denise Jack

Nauru: Brendoski John Limen

Palau: Alfonsa Koshiba and Zoe Kintaro

Papua New Guinea: Magdelyn Kuari and Lorraine Pohakiu

Samoa: Maria Melei and Dahlia Loibl

Solomon Islands: Dalcy Tozaka Ilala

Tonga: Balwyn Faotusia

Tuvalu: Letasi Iulai

Vanuatu: Nancy Wells

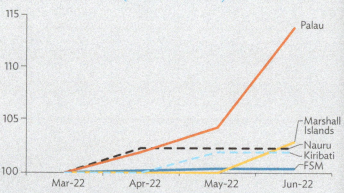

Figure 2: Retail Fuel Price Trends in Micronesia (March 2022 = 100)

FSM = Federated States of Micronesia.
Source: ADB estimates.

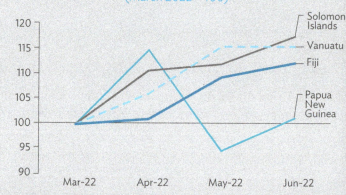

Figure 3: Retail Fuel Price Trends in Melanesia (March 2022 = 100)

Source: ADB estimates.

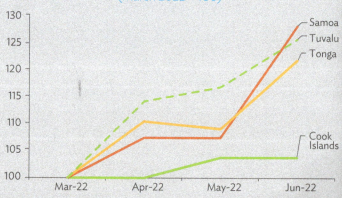

Figure 4: Retail Fuel Price Trends in Polynesia (March 2022 = 100)

Source: ADB estimates.

COUNTRY ECONOMIC ISSUES

Sustaining Fiji's recovery tempo: Role of climate finance amid rising inflation

Lead authors: Isoa Wainiqolo and Noel Del Castillo

Climate change is one of Fiji's significant development challenges. The country has always been subject to natural events such as cyclones. For example, the government estimates that the damage from Tropical Cyclone Winston in 2016 amounted to a fifth of Fiji's gross domestic product (GDP). Aside from cyclones, rising sea levels, increased risk of flooding, and other impacts of climate change are expected to exacerbate the development challenges that the country is already facing. The economic cost of similar disasters will rise over the coming decades.

The government has committed to respond to the threats posed by climate change by investing in long-term strategies that will ensure the country's resilience. As the economy regains its footing and restarts its recovery from coronavirus disease (COVID-19) with the recent reopening of the tourism sector, rolling out Fiji's climate adaptation plans can help sustain the recovery tempo. This will play a vital role in supporting resilience, even as rising inflation is threatening recent economic gains.

RECOVERY AMID RISKS

The economy of Fiji recorded a cumulative 21.3% contraction because of COVID-19 in 2020 and 2021. Fiji recorded its first case in March 2020 although stringent control measures initially limited the spread of the virus. Tax revenue contracted by half and employment by a third because of the shutdown of its tourism industry. With mounting economic costs from the prolonged border shutdown, and following an outbreak in April 2021, Fiji ramped up its vaccination campaign with the support of development partners. By November 2021, the coverage increased to 97% for the first dose and 90% for both doses. This allowed the reopening of Fiji's tourism industry in December 2021. By the end of June 2022, 100% of eligible adult population had received the first dose and more than 97% had received the second dose.

With the benefit of being the first mover ahead of competing tourist destinations such as Bali (Indonesia) and Thailand, Fiji received the highest number of outbound Australian travelers in December 2021 and January 2022. Visitor arrivals for June 2022 were almost 73% of pre–COVID-19 pandemic (June 2019) levels. In terms of source country, the number of Australian tourists was at 97% of the June 2019 levels, Canadian tourists at 80%, American tourists at 78%, and New Zealanders two-thirds of the pre-pandemic figures. However, arrivals in the first half of the year represented only half of comparable 2019 performance (Figure 1).

Based on recent visitor arrivals and forward booking trends, the Fiji economy is now projected to grow by 11.7% in 2022, 8.5% in 2023, and 9.9% in 2024. Tourism-related sectors contribute 10.7 percentage points of the projected 2022 growth rate with spillovers to other sectors of the economy. Tax income, which represented 85% of pre-pandemic government revenue, has also increased. Value-added tax collections (representing 25% of pre-pandemic government revenue) increased by 48% in FY2022, while employment income tax increased by 7% as jobs are gradually being restored.

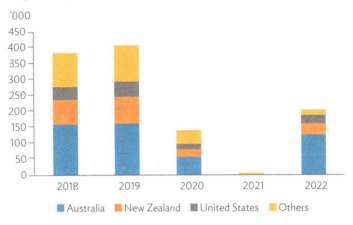

Figure 1: Fiji Visitor Arrivals (January–June), by Source Country

Source: Fiji Bureau of Statistics. Visitor Arrivals Statistics (accessed 1 July 2022).

Figure 2: Drivers of Inflation in Fiji

Source: Fiji Bureau of Statistics. Consumer Price Index (accessed 12 July 2022).

As recovery builds momentum, the impact of the Russian invasion of Ukraine on commodity prices is projected to offset nominal gains in economic activity and revenue collections. Since November 2021, overall consumer prices have increased by 5.7% in a period of 6 months, the highest on record for the same period. The price increases are dominated by food and fuel-related categories (Figure 2). In the first quarter of 2022, the import values of fuel products increased annually by 72%, vegetable products by 41%, and prepared food by 41%, underpinned by both high import prices and improvement in demand conditions. The second-round effects of the increase in prices are also being transmitted downstream. High fuel prices have led to increased bus fares, while higher inflation has necessitated increases in national minimum wages. In its FY2022 revised budget announcement, the government set out phased increases in national minimum wage and indicated possible relative increases in the other sectoral wages.[1]

VULNERABILITY TO DISASTERS

Climate change and rising sea levels pose long-term threats to Fiji's low-lying islands. These areas will be increasingly susceptible to storm surges and flooding and may eventually become unsuitable for settlement, forcing many thousands of people to relocate and resulting in loss of life. The situation is likely to be aggravated further by an increase in the number and intensity of cyclones. Aside from the direct impact on Fiji's population, there will be a recurring threat to Fiji's tourism sector—the destruction of business structures and public infrastructure will have serious economic consequences. Since 2016, four category 5 tropical cyclones have struck Fiji—Cyclones Winston, Gita, Harold, and Yasa—which have resulted in a cumulative damage equivalent to 21.9% of GDP (World Bank 2017a, Boila 2018, Ravuwai 2020, and Talei 2021). The damages inflicted by tropical cyclones and floods also translate into an average of 25,700 Fijians who are being pushed into poverty every year, and this could increase to an annual average of 32,400 Fijians forced into poverty by 2050 (Government of Fiji et al. 2017) (Figure 3). Meanwhile, extreme temperatures and variations in rainfall will affect agricultural output with serious consequences on food security and on households dependent on agricultural income. Like other Pacific countries, Fiji's health system is also vulnerable to the long-term impact of climate change through various diseases brought about by rising temperatures (Government of Fiji et al. 2017).

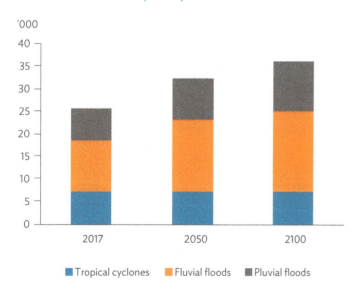

Figure 3: Projected Number of Fijians Falling into Poverty Due to Tropical Cyclones and Floods

Source: Government of Fiji, World Bank, and Global Facility for Disaster Reduction and Recovery. 2017. *Fiji 2017: Climate Vulnerability Assessment - Making Fiji Climate Resilient*. Washington, DC.

BUILDING RESILIENCE

To reduce the country's vulnerability to climate change, the government has identified five priority areas for intervention: (i) pursue better approaches to urban planning, (ii) upgrade infrastructure services, (iii) strengthen the agriculture and fisheries sectors, (iv) conserve ecosystems, and (v) build socioeconomic resilience. The government's assessment indicates that it will need to spend an estimated F$9.3 billion over 10 years, equivalent to 78.3% of its pre-pandemic GDP (2019), to ensure the country's resiliency and adaptability to climate change (Government of Fiji et al. 2017).

Between 2016 and 2019, Fiji's actual investment in climate-related activities averaged F$782 million annually—transport, disaster risk management, and water and sanitation accounted for 85.3% of this expenditure (Government of Fiji 2020). The heavy focus on these sectors is reflective of the reconstruction and recovery efforts that the government undertook to address the damage that Tropical Cyclone Winston inflicted in 2016.

The three sectors continued to dominate Fiji's allocation of climate-related investments in succeeding national budgets. The government allocated a yearly average total of F$201.5 million for climate projects from 2019 to 2021, 89.8% of which went to transport, disaster risk management, and water and sanitation. The transport sector has consistently received the largest allocation, accounting for an average of 65.9% of total projects, highlighting the vulnerability of the sector to climate change and its immediate impact on the population.

The Green Climate Fund (GCF) has short-listed at least two adaptation projects in the housing and blue economy sectors and three mitigation projects in forestry, transport, and energy.[2] Fiji's Ministry of Economy has also identified several other adaptation and mitigation priority projects in the pipeline, with some projects still to secure funding.

SOURCES OF FINANCING

Fiji had explored both domestic and international financing sources for its climate-related projects. In August 2017, it implemented the Environment and Climate Adaptation Levy (ECAL), a tax imposed on specific goods, services, and income. The revenue collected from ECAL is being used to support the government's climate change mitigation and adaptation efforts, as well as disaster relief and response programs. Three months after ECAL took effect, the government issued the first green bond introduced by a developing country—the F$100 million Fiji Sovereign Green Bond. It received strong interest from domestic and international investors, and all bond issuances were oversubscribed. Funds raised from the issuance of the green bonds were used to finance select climate-related projects. Fiji will issue its first blue bond in the latter part of 2022 to help finance ocean-centric undertakings. This will include projects in blue shipping to reduce greenhouse gas emissions; sustainable fisheries to expand aquaculture and protect natural fish stocks threatened by climate change; and sustainable waste management (Kumar 2022).

Fiji has also tapped financing solutions from multilateral banks and bilateral partners. Effective 1 July 2019, the International Development Association (IDA) reclassified Fiji's borrowing status from "International Bank for Reconstruction and Development (IBRD) only" to "Blend," which allows the country to borrow at concessional terms.[3] On 21 February 2020, the government signed a standby loan for disaster recovery and rehabilitation with the Japan International Cooperation Agency (JICA) amounting to ¥5 billion.[4] This was drawn down in two tranches—in May 2020 and in February 2021. The facility can be accessed following the declaration of a natural hazard. Together with ADB support, the concessional facilities lowered government financing costs and helped support government COVID-19 response measures. In November 2021, ADB approved the country grouping reclassification of Fiji from group C to group B, making it eligible for a blend of concessional and regular ordinary capital resources. This is based on Fiji's declining per capita income and limited creditworthiness. On 22 June 2022, ADB approved a $150 million support package, which includes its first concessional lending to Fiji of $60 million to help support economic recovery and build resilience. On 4 July 2022, the World Bank approved a $100 million support package, half of which is through the IDA facility.

Fiji has also gained access to the GCF with direct funding of $36 million for two major projects: the Agrophotovoltaic Project in Ovalau and the Urban Water Supply and Wastewater Management Project the latter in partnership with ADB as GCFs accredited entity. GCF financing mostly focused on the grant component and a small portion of the loan component.

THE ROAD AHEAD

Fiji's groundbreaking Climate Change Act 2021 provides a platform for advancing the climate finance agenda. Section 71 of the act requires that all public infrastructure proposals must undergo a climate risk and resilience assessment prior to securing approval. Section 91 requires the minister for finance, in consultation with the Reserve Bank of Fiji, to develop climate finance strategies, frameworks, and approaches to support and coordinate Fiji's ongoing access to climate finance.

External funds will remain a critical part of budget financing even after the tourism industry recovers. Fiji's future climate financing solutions will require a different financing mix. Considering the high cost of building climate-resilient infrastructure and its recent country grouping reclassification in ADB, Fiji can avail of grants/concessional resources to partly finance such projects. Alternatively, the government can consider cost-sharing mechanisms such as public–private partnerships in line with Section 43 of the act that encourages the involvement of the private sector in climate change mitigation efforts. This may include renewable power generation.

The COVID-19 pandemic has widened the government's budget deficit because stimulus spending was needed to prop up an economy battered by the collapse in tourism. With the deficit expected to further widen this year before moderating in succeeding years, it may be difficult for Fiji to mobilize non-grant resources for its climate adaptation plans. Rising inflation can set back the current economic recovery phase, but the continuous rollout of vital climate-related infrastructure, supported by different financing modalities, can help sustain Fiji's long-term growth prospects.

Endnotes

[1] The review was initially planned for 2020 but was shelved because of COVID-19. As per the amendment, the minimum wage rate will increase from F$2.68 per hour to F$4.00 per hour by 1 January 2023. The four tranches are increase to (i) F$3.01 per hour by 1 April 2022, (ii) F$3.34 per hour by 1 July 2022, (iii) F$3.67 per hour by 1 October 2022, and (iv) F$4.00 per hour by 2023.

[2] The blue economy refers to the "sustainable use of ocean resources for economic growth, improved livelihoods, and jobs while preserving the health of ocean ecosystem" (World Bank 2017b).

[3] Fiji met all four conditions in per capita income below Graduation Discussion Income, limited credit worthiness for accessing commercial credit, constrained by creditworthiness or affordability considerations and the country being highly vulnerable to climatic effects or long-term impact of climate change (International Development Association 2019). In November 2019, the World Bank approved its first Fiji operation using the IDA facility. The $69 million operation comprised IBRD loan ($6 million, maturity = 15 years, grace = 5 years); IDA credit ($29 million, maturity = 40 years, grace = 10 years); and IDA Scale-Up Facility Credit ($29 million, maturity = 30 years, grace = 10 years). IBRD loans refer to loan given at market rates, while IDA loans are at concessional terms.

[4] The loan has a term of 40 years with an interest rate of 0.01% and has a grace period of 10 years (JICA 2020).

References

Boila, S. 2018. TC Gita damage cost stands at $1.23m. *FBC News*. 19 March.

Government of Fiji. 2020. *Fiji Climate Finance Snapshot 2016–2019*. Suva.

Government of Fiji. 2022. *Fiji National Climate Finance Strategy*. Suva.

Government of Fiji, World Bank, and Global Facility for Disaster Reduction and Recovery. 2017. *Fiji 2017: Climate Vulnerability Assessment - Making Fiji Climate Resilient*. Washington, DC: World Bank.

International Development Association. 2019. *Republic of Fiji: Eligibility for Blend Country Borrower Status.* Washington, DC.

Japan International Cooperation Agency (JICA). 2020. Signing of Japanese ODA Loan with Fiji: Contributing to immediate recovery from natural disasters, together with mainstreaming disaster risk. Press release. 21 February.

JICA. 2022. Signing of Japanese ODA Loan Agreement with Fiji: Contributing to the COVID-19 crisis response in Fiji through provision of budget support. Press release. 22 February.

Kumar, W. 2022. Fiji to Launch Blue Bond. *The Fiji Times*. 18 April.

Ravuwai, I. 2020. Estimated Damage from Cyclone Harold is $100M, Minister Says. *Fiji Sun*. 28 May.

Talei, F. 2021. Cyclone Yasa Damage Costs Hit $500m: Seruiratu. *Fiji Sun*. 13 February.

World Bank. 2017a. Resilience & love in action: Rebuilding after Cyclone Winston. News Feature Story. 7 November.

World Bank. 2017b. What is the Blue Economy? Infographic. 6 June.

Assessing the North Pacific's preparedness for sustainable investing

Lead authors: Remrick Patagan, Rommel Rabanal, and Cara Tinio

As the immediate health risks posed by the COVID-19 pandemic recede, policymakers are refocusing attention on challenges such as inclusive growth, sustainability, and resilience. The case for sustainable investing is premised on the shortcomings of financial markets in pricing long-term climate risks. On the one hand, asset owners who rely on market benchmarks may end up investing in carbon-intensive companies that contribute to climate change. This also exposes them to climate transition-related risks such as stranded assets from the repricing and reallocation of investments. On the other hand, a climate-sensitive investment strategy helps avoid those risks and could be used to push for better climate-related governance in carbon-intensive companies.

Among Pacific developing member countries (DMCs), the North Pacific economies (NPEs) are taking the lead in aligning the investment strategies of their public pension and trust funds with their climate goals. All three countries—the Marshall Islands, the Federated States of Micronesia (FSM), and Palau—have national trust funds that are intended as long-term sources of government financing. This article explores the steps that have been taken thus far to incorporate climate and sustainability considerations into investment decisions of their public investment funds and assesses potential issues that need to be addressed to facilitate the transition.

FEDERATED STATES OF MICRONESIA

With rising sea levels and flood risks along with more frequent and intense tropical storms, the FSM recognizes the existential threat posed by climate change and has taken significant steps to address the problem. On the external front, it has engaged in international discussions and pushed for ambitious climate targets and actions alongside other Pacific DMCs. Domestically, the FSM has made progress in its Nationally Determined Contribution (NDC)—a climate action plan to cut emissions and adapt to climate impacts—through the pursuit of renewable energy and efficiency initiatives but significant gaps remain in terms of adaptation and disaster resilience (IMF 2019).

Part of the problem stems from capacity constraints, particularly on planning and implementation at various levels of government, but funding nevertheless remains a primary challenge. The International Monetary Fund (IMF) estimates that the FSM has a public investment financing gap of $400 million–$500 million for its climate initiatives over 2020–2035. This is exacerbated by uncertainty over the potential winding down of Compact-related assistance from the United States in 2023. Alternative sources of long-term financing for general government expenditures have been established, notably the Compact of Free Association Trust Fund (FSM CTF) and the smaller FSM Trust Fund (FSM TF), though their long-term sufficiency has yet to be tested (ADB 2015), and there may be need for increased external grant funding to make up for the financing gap while domestic financing sources are being shored up.

This situation puts the spotlight on the long-term viability of the FSM TF over which the Government of the FSM exercises sole discretion vis-à-vis the FSM CTF where the United States retains majority control. As of end-January 2020, the FSM TF had a total balance of $284.2 million and has recorded investment gains of about $82 million since 2011. As an institutional investor, however, the FSM TF faces exposure risks relating to climate transition. A business-as-usual investment strategy based on standard market benchmarks could lead to the accumulation of high-carbon assets, which would conflict with national goals relating to decarbonization and climate mitigation.

In response to these considerations, the government has decided to align its financial investment strategy with its national climate goals through Public Law (PL) No. 22-06. It has also advocated for the global investment community to consider the same approach using its own experience as an example. Signed on 1 June 2021, PL 22-06 amended the FSM Trust Fund Act by recognizing the existential threat of climate change and incorporating climate considerations in investment risks and opportunities. The FSM TF will redirect investments from high-carbon companies toward supporting decarbonization and emerging technologies such as renewable energy.

In a statement made upon signing of PL22-06, FSM President David Panuelo says the FSM is "... putting our money where our mouths are by mandating that the FSM Trust Fund focus on sustainable investment, by mandating that our financial future be intrinsically tied to our World's environmental prosperity. In real terms, this is possibly the single greatest action our Nation has taken in fighting Climate Change thus far, as we see ourselves move away from investing in corporations that harm the environment to corporations that make peace with nature" (FSM Information Services 2021).

Aside from the direct economic impact of more climate-sensitive investing, synchronizing the FSM's investment strategy with its climate goals strengthens its position as an advocate for climate action. It can further reinforce this position by expanding the approach to other public investment funds, particularly the FSM Social Security Administration, as has been done in Palau. There appears to be scope for this under the existing FSM Social Security Administration charter which empowers its board to manage its investments broadly to maximize returns. As in the case of the FSM TF, with high-level support from both the executive and legislative branches of government, necessary changes to the charter can also be enacted to explicitly incorporate climate considerations into its mandate and expand the scope for allowed investment activities.

PALAU

Like its Pacific peers, Palau is already experiencing various adverse impacts of climate change. Sea levels and air temperature have been steadily increasing over the past few decades (IMF 2021b). Rising sea levels can erode coastal areas which are utilized currently for tourism, agriculture, and other economic activities, while warmer waters can lead to coral bleaching that will be detrimental to Palau's diving sites. Similarly, warmer air temperatures can adversely affect some crop production and possibly reduce labor productivity. In its 2015 Climate Change Policy, the government estimated the economic impacts of climate change to be in the order of between 4% and 20% annually, mainly through losses in tourism revenue as well as in agriculture and fish produce. To address these impacts, the policy aims to (i) strengthen adaptation and resilience, (ii) manage disasters and minimize disaster risk, and (iii) mitigate global climate change by shifting toward a low emissions development path.

Palau's long-term climate change adaptation needs remain sizable. The World Bank estimates the costs of adaptation projects during the decade of the 2020s to reach about 4% of gross domestic product per annum. With climate finance received for adaptation only averaging about 1.5%–1.9% of gross domestic product from 2015 to 2019, mobilizing further financing will be critical over the near to medium term.

Despite having a low direct carbon footprint mainly because of its small economic and population size, Palau is also contributing to global climate change mitigation efforts. It was one of the first countries to ratify the United Nations Framework Convention on Climate Change Paris Agreement, with an NDC outlining 2025 targets to (i) reduce energy sector emissions by 22% (relative to 2005 levels), (ii) increase the share of renewables in energy generation to 45%, and (iii) raise energy efficiency by 35%. Also, the Palau Responsible Tourism Framework of 2016 aligns the country's overall tourism strategy with climate change objectives including emphasis on environmental conservation.

More recently, Palau has also implemented further proactive measures to curb any indirect contribution to global carbon emissions.

In response to an analysis of investments of Pacific sovereign wealth funds—which showed that each $1 million in revenue generated from global capital market investments can be associated with 135 cubic tons of carbon emissions per year—the Palau Social Security Administration (SSA) updated its investment policy in 2021. In October 2021, under a new climate transition investment strategy, the SSA transferred $60 million from its portfolio to climate transition investments that pursue a parallel objective of reducing carbon emissions. The goal is to reduce indirect contributions to global carbon emissions by half (relative to a business-as-usual scenario) through climate-responsive passive investments.

In parallel, the Palau Compact Trust Fund (CTF) became a signatory in July 2021 to the Principles for Responsible Investment (PRI) supported by the United Nations. The PRI is recognized globally as the leading network of asset owners and investment managers that integrates environmental, social, and governance (ESG) issues into their investment decisions. Among the PRI's key principles are incorporating ESG issues into investment analysis and decision-making processes as well as promoting transparency and disclosure through annual reporting on key activities and progress toward implementing responsible investment.

To summarize, both the Palau SSA and CTF have taken the first important steps toward strengthening climate-related investment. This is through the recent integration of climate change mitigation considerations in their strategies and policies, as well as through ongoing efforts to strengthen fiscal governance toward ensuring the sustainability of asset funds. Over the medium to longer term, further refinements to investment strategies as well as to fund mandates (particularly for the CTF) on an as-needed basis, along with sustained efforts to build local capacities for investment management, specializing in climate-related investment portfolios, can help Palau in further mobilizing sovereign wealth funds as another key resource in mitigating climate change.

MARSHALL ISLANDS

The Marshall Islands comprises low-lying atolls and islands with a total land area of 181.3 square kilometers, spread out over almost 2.0 million square kilometers of ocean. High exposure to various natural hazards including droughts, typhoons, ocean acidification, and sea level rise, combined with geographical remoteness and a narrow economic base, mean that the socioeconomic impacts of climate change and disasters significantly constrain the country's resilience to shocks.

Recognizing the significant existential threat posed by climate change, the Marshall Islands is a vocal member of international forums, including the United Nations Framework Convention on Climate Change as well as the Vulnerable Twenty Group of countries most at risk from climate change, calling for decisive collective action. It was the first country to submit an NDC to help mitigate the adverse impacts of climate change in 2015, and the first to submit an enhanced NDC in 2018. This enhanced NDC sets a more ambitious target to reduce greenhouse gas emissions to at least 32% below 2010 levels by 2025 and to at least 45% below 2010 levels by 2030; and commits to a gender-responsive and human rights-based approach in planning, programming, and implementation. A further enhancement in 2020 specified a commitment to reduce greenhouse gas emissions from domestic shipping to 40% below the 2010 levels by 2030, and fully decarbonize the sector by 2050. In 2018, the Marshall Islands also launched its Tile Til Eo 2050 Climate Strategy, which envisions net-zero emissions and 100% renewable energy use by 2050, and commits to developing a national action plan for climate change adaptation and resilience.

These climate change commitments and financing strategies are centered on supporting direct interventions in adaptation and resilience, for which estimated costs are considerable: the IMF (2021) estimates that the country will require $14 million–$42 million a year during this decade, rising to $16 million–$58 million a year by the 2040s, for coastal protection alone. There is no explicit policy yet to integrate ESG into the investment fund decisions of the Trust Fund for the People of the Republic of the Marshall Islands (RMI CFATF). Assets held by the trust fund as of the end of fiscal year 2021 do not show investments in any ESG-oriented assets (RMI CFATF 2022). Further, considering long-standing concerns about unfunded liabilities, the Marshall Islands Social Security Retirement Fund is oriented toward meeting current pensioners' needs without compromising future pensioners' ability to meet their own needs.

However, the Trust Fund Committee has begun exploring an ESG policy for future investments. The Marshall Islands is also working to establish a national climate finance mechanism to help expedite crucial climate action. Among others, this mechanism would help the government manage and maximize climate change-related funds; consider strategic investments in mitigation, adaptation, and resilience; and strengthen internal budgeting, planning, and monitoring systems that could also help integrate ESG into investment fund decisions. The country also recognizes the need to promote private sector investments, particularly in risk mitigation.

Amid the immediate needs to meet adaptation and resilience objectives and to adequately resource future public spending and pension, adopting a sustainable investment approach would be another way for the Marshall Islands to "walk the talk" regarding climate change. National policy has long recognized the need to undertake trade and investment that considers environmental and social concerns (Government of the Marshall Islands 2012). An ESG-aligned investment strategy would contribute to putting these policies into action, ensure that the country does not inadvertently support any initiatives that are not socially compliant, and help boost its moral leadership on responsible climate management.

An examination of the investment advisors engaged with the RMI CFATF shows that they offer advisory services regarding sustainable investment, as well as ESG investment options. Besides keeping the Trust Fund Committee apprised of the CFATF's existing ESG exposure, they could also be tapped to help the country craft a sustainable investment strategy.

ASSESSING READINESS FOR SUSTAINABLE INVESTMENT

The United Nations Environment Programme (2017) has identified best practice considerations to enhance the mobilization of sovereign wealth fund assets for climate-related investments. Table 1 summarizes these considerations and provides an assessment of the status and opportunities for improvement among the NPEs.

Table 1: Evaluating the Mobilization of Sovereign Wealth Funds for Climate-Related Investments

Best practice	Palau SSA	Palau CTF	FSM Trust Fund	RMI CFATF
1. Incorporating climate risk as a long-term financial risk is critical, and the best way to do this is to systematically include climate-related risks and opportunities in strategic asset allocation.	Adopted a climate transition investment strategy, under which $60 million of assets have already been shifted to climate transition investments that pursue the dual objectives of reducing carbon emissions while seeking long-term capital appreciation.	A signatory to the PRI, committing to integrate economic, social, and governance into investment decisions. The CTF Investment Policy Statement was amended in August 2021 explicitly to pursue climate change mitigation objectives, including through Appendix C on Sustainable and Responsive Investment Performance Metrics and Prudent Process toward Climate Change Mitigation.	Under the recently enacted PL 22-06, the fund recognizes the existential threat from climate change, and mandates that investments should follow a sustainable investment policy that integrates climate-related risks and opportunities. Portfolio management is also expected to evolve in conformity with prevailing green finance policies. In particular, the portfolio "shall seek protection from investment risks associated with rapid global decarbonization" and "seek investment opportunities associated with a… transition to lower carbon economy."	The Trust Fund Committee that supervises the CFATF's operation and management is exploring the possibility of an economic, social, and governance policy for future investments. The fund's prevailing Investment Policy Statement states that the broad investment objective is to "maximize investment returns and assets" through to the end of fiscal year 2023, after which it will seek to "produce a level of return sufficient to maintain levels of spending from the Trust Fund consistent with the desires of the members and consistent with risk parameters and spending policy to be defined at that time."

continued on next page

Table 1: continued

Best practice	Palau SSA	Palau CTF	FSM Trust Fund	RMI CFATF
2. To incorporate climate risk in this way also requires revisiting beliefs about the long-term mission of the sovereign wealth fund (SWF) and promoting an understanding among top-level decision-makers of the need to reconcile a long-term investment horizon with long-term climate-related risks and opportunities.	[Not directly applicable as the SSA is a pension fund] The SSA's primary mandate is to ensure that "persons covered may be ensured a measure of security in their old age or during disability, and may be given in old age an opportunity for leisure without hardship and loss of income, and, further, to provide survivor's insurance for their spouses and children", such that pursuing climate-related investments can only be an ancillary objective.	The Palau CTF was established "to assist the Government of Palau in its efforts to advance the well-being of the people of Palau…". As the mandate is broad in scope and the CTF managed exclusively by the Government of Palau, climate change considerations can be implicitly (and perhaps later explicitly) imbued into the CTF's formal mandate.	PL 22-06 also overhauled the purpose of the fund by explicitly including sustainability and the need to address "long-term challenges and… threats" in its long-term mission. There is also considerable buy-in among top officials of the fund and both the executive and legislative branches of the national government as demonstrated by the passage of PL 22-06 and public commitments to long-term sustainability considerations.	The Trust Fund Agreement envisions the CFATF to "contribute to the economic advancement and long-term budgetary self-reliance of the Republic of the Marshall Islands" by supporting expenditures in education and health care (the stated priority sectors), and the environment, among others, as well as other sectors agreed upon by the governments of the Marshall Islands and the United States.
3. Governance plays a fundamental role. The clearer the fiscal rule governing flows in and out of the SWFs is, the easier it will be to design a consistent sustainable-development strategy.	A social security reform bill currently being considered by the Palau national congress aims to restore balance to the long-term contribution–benefit ratio, which was disrupted by recent legislated unfunded benefit adjustments. Among others, the bill would simplify the benefit structure, while retaining the system's progressivity and allowing for inflation-indexed adjustments to pensions to eliminate pressure for any future legislated supplemental benefits. The reforms are expected to reestablish the SSA's long-run financial sustainability.	The Fiscal Responsibility Act passed in November 2021 sets out principles for managing public revenue, expenditure, debt, and fiscal buffers. This includes a provision to preserve the real value of the CTF over time (i.e., effectively transforming it into a perpetual fund from its current state as a sinking fund) by refining investment and withdrawal rules. This will promote the longer-term sustainability of the CTF, and, in combination with the updated investment policy statement, can provide a sustainable vehicle for supporting climate change mitigation through investment allocation decisions.	The fund is structured into a long-term savings Account A and a disbursement Account B; and is governed by fiscal rules meant to safeguard its financial sustainability. PL 22-06 amended Section 1216 of the fund's charter which imposes restrictions on investment activities to reduce risks and incorporates climate risk considerations in its investment strategy. A 2020 performance audit, however, has identified weaknesses in the Fund's governance, internal controls, risk management, and operational processes.	The CFATF has a long-term savings account A, disbursement account B, and buffer account C. The Trust Fund Agreement prescribes rules regarding the use of these accounts to ensure the fund's financial sustainability, but specific details on distribution policy and fiscal rules have yet to be determined.
4. If the SWF has stronger in-house investment capabilities, sustainable investment strategies will be better understood, developed, and implemented.	Supported by foreign professional investment managers in implementing the SSA's new climate transition investment strategy. Building local investment capacity can be a longer-term objective.	Engages foreign professional investment managers as well as a registered investment advisor, who are now guided by the updated investment policy statement that explicitly pursues climate change mitigation objectives through asset allocations. Building local investment capacity can be a longer-term objective.	The fund engages a major investment management firm as its investment advisor, which is a PRI signatory and provides advisory services on the integration of sustainability risks in investment processes. Building stronger in-house investment capacity on sustainable investment is necessary to avoid over-reliance on the Investment advisor and exercise effective monitoring and management.	The CFATF engages professional investment advisors and money managers to invest the fund in a diversified asset portfolio. The current investment advisor, engaged by the fund since 2017, and money managers are PRI signatories. Given the long-standing capacity constraints, building in-house capacity for sustainable investment will be a challenge.

CTF = Compact of Free Association Trust Fund, FSM = Federated States of Micronesia, PL 22-06 = Public Law 22-06, PRI = Principles for Responsible Investment, RMI CFATF = Trust Fund for the People of the Republic of the Marshall Islands, SSA = Social Security Administration.
Sources: Government of the Federated States of Micronesia, Government of the Marshall Islands, and Government of Palau.

CONCLUSION

Owing to their extreme vulnerability and negligible contributions to climate change, Pacific DMCs are ideally positioned to provide moral leadership in advocating for the necessary actions needed to meet the goals under the Paris Agreement. By "walking the talk" on incorporating climate risk considerations into their financial investment decisions as demonstrated in the North Pacific, wider adoption in the rest of the region can strengthen the Pacific's position as a beacon for climate action and expand their influence toward this end.

All three NPEs show some degree of readiness for undertaking sustainable investment, mostly in terms of having strong investment capacity through the service providers engaged by their respective funds. The FSM and Palau have taken more concrete action in implementing the other areas of best practice by specifically espousing investment policies with ESG considerations and establishing firmer rules on the governance of their funds, while the Marshall Islands is still exploring an ESG policy and working to determine the CFATF's distribution policy and fiscal procedures consistent with the Trust Fund Agreement (RMI CFATF 2022).

Issues may arise in the implementation of sustainable investment policies so related rules and regulations must be clear and well-enforced to ensure consistency with stated positions on climate risk. The rules governing pension and sovereign wealth funds also need to be well-defined, and flexibilities may need to be limited to avoid excessive drawdowns that would compromise their future viability. Finally, a challenge common to all NPEs is the lack of local in-house investment capacity. Although this is partly offset by the engagement of professional investment advisors, developing this capacity is still needed to maintain appropriate oversight and control over investment processes.

References

Asian Development Bank. 2015. *Trust Funds and Fiscal Risks in the North Pacific: Analysis of Trust Fund Rules and Sustainability in the Marshall Islands and the Federated States of Micronesia.* October.

Embassy of the Federated States of Micronesia. 2021. *President Panuelo Advocates for Aligning Investment Strategies to National Climate Goals.* Press Release. 22 October.

FSM Congress. 2021. *Public Law No. 22-06.* 1 June.

FSM Information Services. 2020. *The FSM Trust Fund's Current Balance is $284,200,000.* Press Release. 8 March.

FSM Information Services. 2021. *President Panuelo Signs Public Law Amending & Strengthening the FSM Trust Fund; The Trust Fund is Now Mandated to Address Climate Change, Focus on Renewable & Green Energy, Thereby Aligning the FSM's Sovereign Fund with Our Environmental Values of Green & Low Carbon Investment.* Press Release. 9 June.

FSM Legal Information System. *Chapter 12: FSM Trust Fund. Code of the Federated States of Micronesia* (accessed 21 June 2022).

FSM Office of the National Public Auditor. 2021. *Actions are required to effectively and efficiently achieve the goals of the FSM Trust Fund.* Report No. 2021-02.

Government of the Marshall Islands. 2020. *Updated Communication on the Marshall Islands Paris Agreement NDC.* Majuro.

Government of the Marshall Islands, Ministry of Resources and Development. 2012. *The Trade Policy for the Republic of the Marshall Islands.* Majuro.

Government of the Marshall Islands, National Disaster Management Office. Country profile.

Government of the Marshall Islands, Office of Commerce, Investment and Tourism. 2019. *RMI Investment Policy Statement.* Majuro.

Government of Palau. 2015. *Palau Climate Change Policy for Climate-Resilient and Low Emissions Development.* Koror.

Ingram, D. Empowering institutional investors to make climate-responsive decisions. *Financial Times* (Partner Content).

International Monetary Fund (IMF). 2019. Federated States of Micronesia: Climate Change Policy Assessment. *IMF Staff Country Reports.* 6 September.

IMF. 2021a. *Republic of the Marshall Islands: 2021 Article IV Consultation—Press Release; Staff Report; and Statement by the Executive Director for the Republic of the Marshall Islands.* Washington, DC.

IMF. 2021b. *Republic of Palau: 2021 Article IV Consultation—Press Release; Staff Report; and Statement by the Executive Director for the Republic of Palau* (Appendix I: Palau's Climate Change Challenges), based on data from the National Climatic Data Center (noaa.gov).

Marshall Islands Social Security Administration. About Us.

NDC Partnership. 2019. *Marshall Islands takes next steps on national climate finance mechanism.* 17 June.

Regional NDC Pacific Hub. Marshall Islands (Republic of) (accessed 23 June 2022).

Trust Fund for the People of the Republic of the Marshall Islands. News & Events.

Trust Fund for the People of the Republic of the Marshall Islands. 2022. *Fiscal Year 2021 Annual Report.*

United Nations Environment Programme. 2017. *Financing sustainable development: the role of sovereign wealth funds for green investment.* Working paper. December.

Climate finance and water security in Kiribati and Tuvalu

Lead authors: Noel Del Castillo, Lily-Anne Homasi, and Isoa Wainiqolo

Kiribati and Tuvalu are two of the most vulnerable countries to climate change with the availability of potable water becoming a major concern. Both atoll countries are situated just a few meters above sea level, and are already particularly susceptible to tidal waves triggered by tropical cyclones that may cause flooding for days and contaminate drinking water. Any rise in sea levels because of climate change would increase the damage caused by such events. Similarly, prolonged drought can deplete water supplies, which can then lead to serious shortages and associated health issues. Access to safe drinking water has become one of the major concerns of these two countries, necessitating its inclusion in their respective climate adaptation policies.

Efforts to improve access to safe water involve building water harvesting infrastructure and strengthening mechanisms for broader water resource management. These economies do not have the fiscal resources to finance the costs of such projects and programs. In this regard, development partners provide a vital source of additional financing. Assessing and understanding the effectiveness of climate financing in improving water security in Kiribati and Tuvalu can offer insights to accelerate efforts.

KIRIBATI

Water security is an important component of Kiribati's climate adaptation plan. Water supply in Kiribati is mostly dependent on rainwater collection and groundwater. As both are highly dependent on rainfall replenishment, prolonged periods of drought place strain on groundwater resources and terrestrial ecosystems, posing direct risks to human health as well as indirectly impacting on subsistence agriculture and, consequently, on food security. Weather and rainfall patterns have become more erratic because of the climate change problem and this, in turn, has translated into more frequent, longer, and more intense drought events. Below-normal rainfall in recent months has resulted in high salinity levels in key water sources and, on 13 June 2022, the government declared a State of Disaster for the entire country.

As Kiribati only has a maximum elevation of 3–4 meters above sea level, tidal waves can easily cause flooding, making groundwater vulnerable to saline contamination. Such has been the case for many i-Kiribati who had to deal with contaminated wells. Many communities use groundwater from wells for drinking, cooking, and farming needs. Although this water is harnessed to some extent, it is brackish and contaminated by animal and human waste, specifically in urban areas (ADB 2021). Contamination by seawater increases the risk of waterborne diseases which makes it unsafe for human consumption. In particular, many babies can suffer from infantile diarrhea—a contributor to infant mortality in Kiribati, which is the highest in the Pacific at 43 deaths per thousand live births (World Bank 2017).

Aside from the direct impacts of climate change, there are other factors that threaten water security in Kiribati. For example, in urbanized areas, where there is increasing demand for fresh water, industrial contamination, such as leakages from diesel power generators, can further reduce the supply of fresh water. Similarly, the continuous tensions and conflicts between affected communities and the government because of declaration of water reserves in privately owned land weakens efforts to increase water supply.[1] Reducing the relatively high network leaks offers an immediate and practical solution in improving piped water supply to households. Ensuring an effective approach to address water security, then, requires not only investment in physical infrastructure but also in programs that will create an enabling legal and communal environment.

Increasing water and food security is one of the 12 major strategies that the Government of Kiribati (2019) identified in the Kiribati Joint Implementation Plan for Climate Change and Disaster Risk Management. There are five key national adaptation priorities that the government enumerated under water security:

(i) "Strengthen national water governance so all key stakeholders are enabled to perform their allocated functions in a coordinated manner to address all water issues, including the impacts of climate change, climate variability and natural disasters;
(ii) Provide efficient harvesting systems and innovative solutions to water availability issues (water availability, quality and quantity);
(iii) Enhance support and enforcement of regulations for water security and safety issues;
(iv) Strengthen communities' engagement in safeguarding water sources and improving water systems; and
(v) Ensure access to improved sanitation facilities, including monitoring the impacts of pollution sources." (Government of Kiribati n.d., p. 14)

One of the targets set by the government in the country's 20-year development plan is to extend access to potable water to 75% of households in 2019 and achieve universal household access by 2023 (Government of Kiribati 2016). While the possibility of achieving this target remains to be seen, Kiribati still needs to address other concerns in water and sanitation to achieve water security. In 2020, ADB released the fourth edition of the Asian Water Development Outlook, which assessed the water security situation of its member countries in Asia and the Pacific across five key dimensions: (i) rural household water security, (ii) economic water security, (iii) urban water security, (iv) environmental water security, and (v) water-related disaster security. Out of a perfect score of 100, Kiribati posted an average national water security (NWS) score of 46.6 in the last three rounds of assessment (Figure 4), among the lowest in the Pacific (Figure 5). The rating it received in 2013 remained the same in 2016 though it improved in the 2020 assessment by 2.4 points, benefiting from a huge boost in the environmental water security dimension. However, it suffered a downgrade in the urban water security dimension in 2020, which is likely reflective of the problems associated with high population density in Tarawa amid weak water and sanitation infrastructure.

Figure 4: National Water Security Scores of Kiribati and Tuvalu

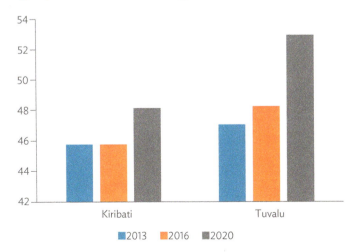

Note: Score out of 100.

Source: ADB. 2020. *Asian Water Development Outlook 2020: Advancing Water Security across Asia and the Pacific.* Manila.

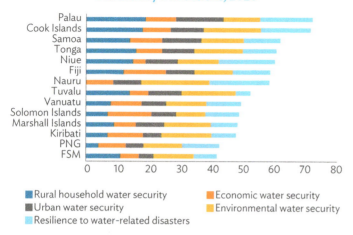

Figure 5: National Water Security Scores of Pacific DMCs Across Key Dimensions, 2020

- Rural household water security
- Urban water security
- Resilience to water-related disasters
- Economic water security
- Environmental water security

DMC = developing member country, FSM = Federated States of Micronesia, PNG = Papua New Guinea.

Notes: Score out of 100. Nauru has no score in Rural Household Water Security because it is a 100% urban state. The National Water Security Index has been determined by multiplying the sum of the other key dimensions by a factor of 5/4.

Source: ADB. 2020. *Asian Water Development Outlook 2020: Advancing Water Security across Asia and the Pacific.* Manila.

In line with its commitments under the Kiribati 20-Year Vision and the 2014 Climate Change Policy, the government, with support from development partners, established the Climate Finance Division under the Ministry of Finance and Economic Development in 2016. Its main role is focused on securing financing to support climate change and disaster risk management (CCDRM) projects. Given the high cost of such projects, external sources of funding are an important component of financing in Kiribati. Between 2011 and 2018, the government accessed $57.1 million for CCDRM projects (Government of Kiribati 2020), most of which came from multilateral development partners, with ADB accounting for the largest share at 27%, followed by the World Bank at 23%, and the European Union at 17%. The water and sanitation sector received the largest share of funding at 40% of total CCDRM expenditure, followed by energy at 19% and transport and infrastructure at 12%. Most of the funding was for adaptation (46.4%) and mitigation (35.4%) with a small amount for disaster risk reduction and management.[2]

One of the biggest water-related infrastructure projects that is being rolled out in Kiribati is the South Tarawa Water Supply Project. The $61.8 million project, which is supported by ADB, the World Bank, and the GCF, aims to improve access to safe climate-resilient water supplies. It will support the delivery of key outputs of the project: (i) provide a climate-resilient and low-carbon water supply infrastructure; (ii) increase the capacity of the Ministry of Infrastructure and Sustainable Energy and the Public Utilities Board to manage water supply infrastructure effectively; (iii) raise awareness of climate change and water, sanitation, and hygiene issues; and (iv) ensure efficient and effective management of project implementation. The project has been hampered by the COVID-19 pandemic. Supply disruptions and inflationary pressures continue to pose as key implementation challenges. Ongoing engagement of key agencies and stakeholders will be critical to manage expectations and the success of improving water security in Kiribati.

TUVALU

Tuvalu is highly dependent on rainfall collection for its supply of fresh water. Although groundwater is available, it is often brackish and unsafe for human consumption. The impacts of climate variability and climate change have exacerbated the challenges faced by Tuvaluans regarding water security. Prolonged periods of drought experienced in 1999 and 2011 pushed the government to declare a state of emergency as supplies of potable water in some of the communities were depleted (Government of Tuvalu 2013). The El Niño Southern Oscillation contributes to high variability in rainfall, and is playing a major role in the severity and incidence of droughts.

Tuvalu's vulnerability to climate change stems primarily from its geographical layout. As a smaller island nation composed of nine atolls, its islands have an average height above sea level of less than 3 meters. Aside from the threat posed by prolonged droughts on its water supply, Tuvalu must cope with tropical cyclones, which can create storm surges, and rising sea levels as a result of climate change. Both can lead to seawater inundation, with contamination of the few remaining groundwater sources. Similarly, rising sea levels and extreme tropical cyclones can also increase the risks of damage to water supply infrastructure and put further strain on the country's already scarce water resources.

In response to the water crisis in 2011, the government has developed a 10-year Water and Sanitation Policy, which is consistent with the national development plans and climate change policy. Aside from improving access to safe water sources, the policy looked at the governance and community management of water and sanitation, and identified sources of financing for such projects. In 2020, water-specific projects represented 8.0% of capital outlays and the ratio is projected to decline to 2.2% in 2022.

Since the water crisis in 2011, government has improved water security in Tuvalu. Based on ADB's (2020a) Asian Water Development Outlook assessment, the country has steadily improved in the last three rounds of its NWS assessment (Figure 4). From an NWS score of 47.1 points in 2013, it achieved 53.0 points in 2021 buoyed by high scores in the key dimensions of rural household water security and environmental water security. Tuvalu is one of the top gainers among ADB member countries as its score improved by 4 points in the environmental water security dimension between the 2013 and 2020 assessment. Despite this, Tuvalu's ranking in the Pacific subregion remains low at eighth place, requiring more improvement in the dimensions of economic water security and water-related disaster security (Figure 5). The water scarcity in Tuvalu requires investment in storage and production facilities. This ties in with Tuvalu's high vulnerability to drought and flooding and, consequently, weak performance in water-related disaster security dimension. OECD (2019) estimates that the total annual investment required to achieve universal access to safely managed water and sanitation services in Tuvalu is equivalent to $350,000 or 1.3% of gross domestic product over the period 2015–2030.

The government has an ongoing and a potential project in its pipeline that will address the country's water security challenge. In partnership with the Global Climate Change Alliance Plus Initiative and the Pacific Community, the Government of Tuvalu has rolled-out a project that aims to improve the supply, storage, and distribution of potable water to communities and schools in Funafuti. The project's key deliverables include purchase of a portable, solar-powered desalination plant, refurbishing the water systems in two primary schools, procuring a 10,000-liter water truck, and national coordination of the project activities. The project is anticipated to be completed by the end of 2022. Meanwhile, ADB approved a project readiness financing for the Funafuti Water and Sanitation Project in June 2020. With potential additional financing from the Global Environment Fund, the project intends to increase access to safe water, improve sanitation, and lower the incidence of waterborne diseases.

FINANCING THE GAP

There are three main sources to finance water-related investments: (i) revenues from water tariffs, (ii) government taxes, and (iii) transfers from development partners. For most of the developing member countries in the subregion, taxes are the primary source of funding water- and sanitation-related infrastructure (ADB 2020a). Using revenues from water tariffs to finance water-related investments is feasible in countries that have sufficiently large customer bases. Recently, there are other modalities of financing water-related investments being explored, such as OECD's (2019) study on mobilizing commercial finance through a blended finance approach. Yet, in many Pacific countries such as Kiribati and Tuvalu, inadequate fiscal resources and small populations frequently push these countries to continue depending heavily on development partner support. Heightened vulnerability of Pacific developing member countries to climate change amid fiscal constraints has further raised the importance of external financing. This has necessitated the entry of climate-specific global funds, such as the GCF, joining conventional development partners to provide funding for big-ticket water infrastructure projects.

The national adaptation plans for climate change that the governments of Kiribati and Tuvalu prepared clearly indicate that water security is a priority. However, to provide stronger impetus to the urgency of addressing water security, there is a need to focus on evidence-based adaptation plans, updated data, and detailed project implementation arrangements, which is expounded below:

- The plans are rich in enumerating strategies that respective governments intend to undertake. But, without clear baseline figures and detailed work plans, it would be difficult to assess the milestones already achieved and the efficacy of the projects carried out.
- Data availability is a vital component in assessing the impact of the intervention. It can also expedite mobilizing support of development partners because it can clearly gauge the significance of its participation. The latest Asian Water Development Outlook likewise highlighted the problems associated with data gaps. It creates constraints in assessing economic water security; prevents independent examination of data to discover new approaches to better water management and security; and weakens efforts for a proactive disaster risk management, diminishing resiliency to water-related disasters (ADB 2020a).
- Detailed implementation arrangements with a dedicated project team are equally important to ensure a smooth project execution. Implementation plans need to be detailed to provide clear guidance on the roles that relevant stakeholders need to perform. Meanwhile, scarcity of technical experts can seriously affect the quality of the project outcome.

Although a substantial share of climate financing has been allocated to improve water security in Kiribati and Tuvalu, difficulties in accessing potable water persists because of delays in project implementation. Limited absorptive capacity prevents these countries from implementing projects efficiently and effectively. The impact of the COVID-19 pandemic and inflation pressures stemming from the Russian invasion of Ukraine exacerbate these problems. Improving water security in Kiribati and Tuvalu should not only involve financing the relevant infrastructure projects, but should also ensure that the necessary project management, public financial management, and other governance support mechanisms are in place.

Endnotes

[1] Landowners are evicted from the subject property and affected communities lose a local amenity when the government prohibits some traditional land uses on the property once it becomes a water reserve (Metutera et al. 2007).

[2] There are several attempts to calculate the climate financing needs of Kiribati. An OECD (2019) study modestly estimated that Kiribati needs to invest at least $1.7 million, equivalent to 1.6% of GDP, annually over the period 2015–2030 to achieve universal access to safely managed water and sanitation services. Meanwhile, a United Nations Development Programme study in 2014, cited in Kiribati's Climate Change Policy document, found that addressing issues arising from poor water and sanitation cost the government and affected households up to $8.3 million annually (Government of Kiribati n.d.).

References

ADB. 2016. *Asian Water Development Outlook 2016: Strengthening Water Security in Asia and the Pacific*. Manila.

ADB. 2020a. *Asian Water Development Outlook 2020: Advancing Water Security across Asia and the Pacific*. Manila.

ADB. 2020b. *Project Administration Manual: South Tarawa Water Supply Project*. Manila.

ADB. 2021. *Climate Change, Water Security, and Women: A Study on the Boiling Water in South Tarawa, Kiribati*. Manila.

Government of Kiribati. 2016. *Kiribati 20-Year Vision 2016-2036*. Tarawa.

Government of Kiribati. 2019. *Kiribati Joint Implementation Plan for Climate Change and Disaster Risk Management 2019–2028.* Tarawa.

Government of Kiribati. 2020. *Kiribati Climate Change and Disaster Risk Finance Assessment Final Report.* Tarawa.

Government of Kiribati. n.d. *Kiribati Climate Change Policy.* Tarawa.

Government of Tuvalu. 2012. *Tuvalu National Strategic Action Plan for Climate Change and Disaster Risk Management.* Funafuti.

Government of Tuvalu. 2013. *Fakanofonofoga Mo Vai Mote Tumaa – Sustainable and Integrated Water and Sanitation Policy 2012-2021.* Funafuti.

Government of Tuvalu. 2021. *TE KANIVA: Tuvalu Climate Change Policy.* Funafuti.

Metutera, T., T. Falkland, and I. White. 2007. *National Integrated Water Resource Management Diagnostic Report Kiribati.*

Organisation for Economic Co-operation and Development (OECD). 2019. *Estimating Investment Needs and Financing Capacities for Water Supply and Sanitation in Asia-Pacific.* Background paper for the Roundtable on Financing Water 5th Meeting. 26–27 November, p. 4.

OECD. 2019. *Making Blended Finance Work for Water and Sanitation: Unlocking Commercial Finance for SDG 6. OECD Studies on Water.* Paris.

World Bank. 2017. Water, water, everywhere, but not a drop to drink: Adapting to life in climate change-hit Kiribati. Feature story. 21 March.

World Bank. 2021a. *Climate Risk Country Profile: Kiribati.* Washington, DC.

World Bank. 2021b. *Climate Risk Country Profile: Tuvalu.* Washington, DC.

Climate adaptation and budgeting amid volatile revenue in Nauru

Lead authors: Jacqueline Connell and Prince Cruz

Nauru is highly exposed to the adverse effects of climate change. The population, concentrated along a narrow coastline, is exposed to rising sea levels; while its oceanic tuna stocks, which supply about 27% of government revenue through fishing license fees and royalties, may be affected by rising ocean temperatures. Nauru is implementing adaptation and mitigation projects to improve its economic and climate resilience. Further work is needed to integrate adaptation plans into the budget framework. Determining the optimal spending on climate-resilient infrastructure—both capital investment and recurrent maintenance spending—is a key policy challenge, and one that is complicated by volatile and uncertain revenues.

Lessening the risks from rising sea levels has been a focus of Nauru's adaptation efforts. Even though much of the 21-square kilometer land area is elevated, this higher ground, known locally as Topside, has been damaged by phosphate mining, leaving it barren and uninhabitable. Consequently, the population and infrastructure, including the government administration and airport, are mostly clustered along a narrow coastline less than 5 meters above sea level (Government of Nauru 2019a). To protect the shoreline, the budget for fiscal year (FY) 2023 (ends 30 June 2023) allocates funding for the continued construction of a 500-meter sea wall.

There are other plans to protect against rising sea levels. The Higher Ground Initiative aspires to transform Nauru's higher grounds into habitable and arable land to enable infrastructure and communities to relocate there (Government of Nauru 2022b). The FY2023 budget allocates A$3.0 million ($2.2 million) to scope options and develop a plan, though the cost of the potential land rehabilitation and infrastructure investment required for a relocation would be far more substantial. As the National Sustainable Development Strategy points out, the process could span generations (Government of Nauru 2019b).

While adaptation requires long-term efforts, Nauru's climate mitigation projects are well progressed. The ADB-funded Solar Power Development Project is expected to raise the energy generation from renewable sources from 3% to 47% upon completion (ADB 2019). This is likely to have outsized benefits for Nauru, which has relied on diesel imports for both energy generation and water desalination. Fuel accounted for an average of 58.4% of imports from 2018 to 2020 (Figure 6). This import dependence exposes Nauru to rising commodity prices and could result in imported inflation if fuel prices remain elevated.

Figure 6: Nauru Imports

Fuel accounted for almost 60% of Nauru's imports.

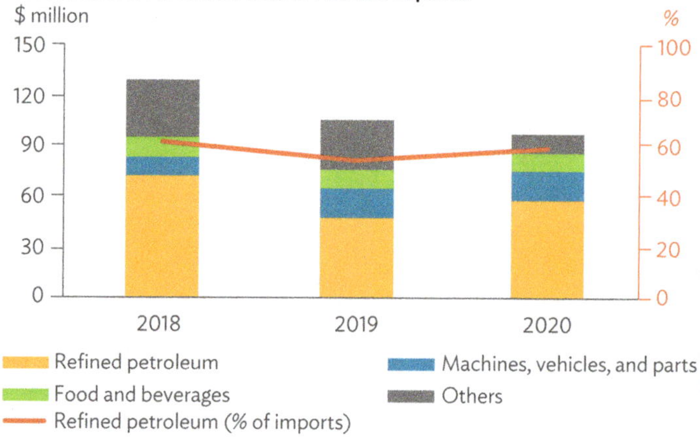

- Refined petroleum
- Machines, vehicles, and parts
- Food and beverages
- Others
- Refined petroleum (% of imports)

Sources: Observatory of Economic Complexity and ADB estimates.

To support mitigation and adaptation measures, the government established the Department of Climate Change and National Resilience in 2020. Earlier, it had approved a national adaptation plan, RONAdapt in 2015, and the Nauru Integrated Infrastructure Strategy in 2019, which identifies priority infrastructure investments, rehabilitation, upgrades, and maintenance. Although the FY2023 fiscal strategy is partly linked to these priorities, further efforts are needed to integrate adaptation and mitigation projects into the government's medium-term budget planning.

Another challenge is that Nauru's budgets do not include forward-year estimates. Revenues related to the Regional Processing Centre (RPC), the largest source of revenue, have been difficult to predict as they are dependent on agreements with the Government of Australia. The lack of a medium-term budget framework makes it difficult to determine the fiscally-sustainable level of government expenditure. This dilemma is particularly acute for climate-resilient infrastructure which tends to require higher upfront investment, compared to standard infrastructure, but has potential to reduce other expenditure in the future (IMF 2021).

The Government of Nauru consistently targets a balanced budget and does not issue debt instruments. In recent years, revenues exceeded budget estimates because of extensions to the RPC and strong demand for fishing licenses (Figure 7). Much of the surplus was channeled into higher expenditure through supplementary budgets.

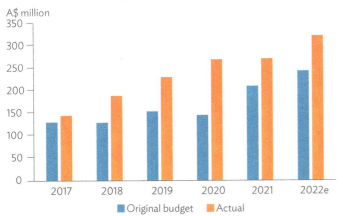

Figure 7: Nauru Original Budget versus Actual Revenues

Revenues have consistently exceeded budget estimates.

e = estimate.
Notes: Revenues as defined by the budget which includes grants, dividends, and loans. Years are fiscal years that end in June of the same year.
Sources: Nauru Ministry of Finance budget documents and ADB estimates.

Despite the large fiscal expansion, the government has built its savings in cash deposits to provide a fiscal buffer and contributed about 10% of revenue to the Nauru Intergenerational Trust Fund. It also paid down debt and reached settlement with creditors (Figure 8). This has improved fiscal and debt sustainability.

These steps have also reduced the risks posed by a potential decline in future revenue. The FY2022 budget indicates that the RPC will transition to an "enduring capability" arrangement in 2023. Nauru will receive a hosting fee from the Government of Australia in return for maintaining the facility capable of being scaled up. However, although the first-year revenue receipts are largely confirmed, the medium-term outlook remains unclear (Government of Nauru 2022a).

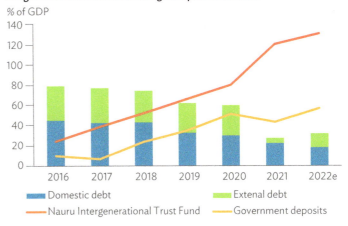

Figure 8: Nauru Public Debt and Financial Assets

The government has built its savings and paid down debt.

e = estimate, GDP = gross domestic product.
Note: Years are fiscal years that end in June of the same year.
Sources: ADB estimates and International Monetary Fund. 2022. *Republic of Nauru 2021 Article IV Consultation - Press Release; Staff Report.* Washington, DC.

If the predictability of revenue improves, Nauru could introduce forward-year budget estimates. These would help decision makers assess the trade-offs between spending more now (including on climate-resilient infrastructure) and saving. If revenues remain robust, Nauru could potentially pool more in the Nauru Intergenerational Trust Fund, which is intended to build a sufficient principal value that can provide future development financing for investments in public infrastructure, environment, health, and education. If revenues fall significantly, however, expenditure will need to be reduced.

While development partners are financing much of the upfront investment in Nauru's climate-resilient infrastructure, recurring spending is needed to maintain those assets over their lifetime. Lack of adequate funding for asset maintenance and repairs has been one of the main reasons for premature infrastructure failures (Government of Nauru 2019a). Ensuring that maintenance is budgeted for and implemented will be critical to make sure that those assets improve Nauru's long-term economic and climate resilience, as intended.

As much of Nauru's climate-resilient infrastructure will be managed by state-owned enterprises (SOEs), continued strengthening of their governance and performance is crucial. SOE revenues need to be adequate to fund maintenance spending. In 2020, the government introduced compensation for SOEs which were tasked with community service obligations such as keeping prices low or providing nonrevenue services (Government of Nauru 2022). Continued monitoring of SOE performance is needed to ensure that these public resources are used efficiently. Institutional reforms to improve SOE performance, such as those undertaken by the power and water utility, would also help safeguard Nauru's investments in climate-resilient infrastructure.

References

ADB. 2019. *ADB, Nauru Sign Grant Agreement for New Solar Project.* Manila.

Government of Nauru. 2015. *Republic of Nauru Framework for Climate Change Adaptation and Disaster Risk Reduction.* Yaren.

Government of Nauru. 2019a. *Nauru Integrated Infrastructure Strategic Plan.* Yaren.

Government of Nauru. 2019b. *Nauru's National Sustainable Development Strategy 2019–2030.* Yaren.

Government of Nauru. 2022a. *Republic of Nauru 2022–23 Budget: Budget Paper No. 1.* Yaren.

Government of Nauru. 2022b. *Republic of Nauru 2022–23 Budget: Budget Paper No. 2.* Yaren.

International Monetary Fund. 2021. *Fiscal Policies to Address Climate Change in Asia and the Pacific.* Washington, DC.

International Monetary Fund. 2022. *Republic of Nauru 2021 Article IV Consultation - Press Release; Staff Report; Informational Annex; and Statement by the Executive Director for Nauru.* Washington, DC.

Fiscal challenges of climate financing in Papua New Guinea

Lead authors: Magdelyn Kuari and Cara Tinio

Papua New Guinea (PNG) is prone to many natural hazards, which are expected to become more frequent and intense with climate change and bring about more serious socioeconomic impacts. Experiences during the 1997 and 2015 drought and frost and the 2018 earthquake in the Hela province show that climate change and natural hazards can also significantly affect the PNG economy and strain government resources. Much of the critical infrastructure in PNG is at risk from future sea level rise, storm surge, flooding, and drought. Competing priorities limit the resources that the country can invest in climate change adaptation or building fiscal buffers to prepare for extreme events. Macroeconomic policies and capital investment programs need to incorporate disaster and climate change resilience, and government capacity to set policy and coordinate climate change efforts must be strengthened.

PNG'S DISASTER VULNERABILITY

PNG is vulnerable to climatic and disaster shocks such as earthquakes, volcanic eruptions, tsunamis, and storm surges. With climate change, floods, landslides, droughts, frost, coastal erosion, and sea level rise are expected to become more frequent and severe. These events result in loss of human life, displacement of the population, damage to infrastructure, more food insecurity, and increases in the prevalence of waterborne diseases.

Historically, PNG has experienced cases of El Niño effects of drought and frost, affecting mostly the rural hinterlands. Early in 1997, the country was hit by Cyclone Justine, which destroyed young cocoa pods and coconut; and widespread drought and frost from an El Niño event, which lasted from March 1997 to early 1998. These twin disasters caused food shortages and affected an estimated 1.2 million people. The drought also reduced water levels, reducing the quality of drinking water and causing more waterborne diseases. In urban households and institutions in particular, interruptions in water and power supply upset normal operations for schools, prisons, hospitals, and small urban centers in impacted provinces. Bushfires caused by the prolonged dry weather damaged gardens and shut down operation of rural airstrips. In addition, the Ok Tedi copper mine was forced to close for 8 months because lower water levels of the Fly River constrained movement of the barges transporting copper concentrates and other supplies for the mine township in PNG's Western Province, and lower water levels at the Porgera mine's reservoir caused a 45-day shutdown. Agriculture exports, particularly cocoa, palm oil, copra, and copra oil, were also affected; only coffee crops showed some resistance to drought.

PNG was hit by another El Niño event between mid-2015 and late 2016, earlier than anticipated. The impact was generally similar to that of the 1997 event, but less severe. The Ok Tedi mine was closed for 7 months and Porgera mine for 16 days to conserve water (RNZ 2015b).

In February 2018, PNG was struck by a 7.2 magnitude earthquake that hit four provinces in PNG's highland region, which host the country's liquefied natural gas and oil fields and the Ok Tedi mine. The earthquake seriously disrupted mining, and petroleum and gas production, damaging the Hides Gas Condensation Plant for the liquefied natural gas project, oil processing facilities, and the Porgera mine's gas and electricity infrastructure. The earthquake also triggered a landslide and destroyed water sources and crops. According to the World Health Organization, 554,000 people were affected by the disaster, with 180,000 people displaced. Key infrastructures, including airfields, bridges, and roads, were damaged and health facilities were closed.

ECONOMIC AND FISCAL IMPACT

As a small, open, and less-diversified economy, PNG's vulnerability to climatic and disaster shocks increases the risks of macroeconomic instability, with implications for the government's poverty reduction efforts. More than 80% of PNG's population lives in rural areas and depends on farming for subsistence and income. The country also relies heavily on exports from the extractive mining, petroleum, and gas sectors as well as agriculture, fishery, and forestry. These sectors combined contributed 45% of PNG's GDP (Papua New Guinea National Statistical Office 2021; Figure 9) and 62% of foreign exchange inflows in 2019 (Bank of Papua New Guinea 2021). According to the Extractive Industry Transparency Initiative 2019 report, the extractive sectors contributed 28% to overall state revenue (excluding salaries and wages tax) in 2019 and employed more than 10,000 PNG nationals.

The impacts of the various disasters have contributed to the volatility of growth. The economy was estimated to have contracted by 6.3% in 1997, with negative growth in both agriculture and industry linked to the drought (ADB 1998). More recently, the impacts of the 2015 drought reduced growth by more than half from a peak of 13.5% in 2014, while the 2018 earthquake contributed to an economic contraction of 0.3%.

Although increasing international prices on its export commodities can help insulate the Government of PNG's revenues from the impact of disasters, emergency response and post-disaster reconstruction and rehabilitation push up public spending. After 2 years of realizing fiscal surpluses, in 1997 the government incurred a fiscal deficit equivalent to 0.5% of GDP as recurrent spending spiked by 32.7% year-on-year (in contrast, current revenues rose by only 13.0%). Between 2015 and 2017, the decline in revenue was equivalent to 2.6% of GDP annually (Figure 10), while the fiscal deficit was the equivalent of 4.0% of GDP a year (Figure 11). Although development partners provided considerable support, the government needed to cut parts of the recurrent and capital investment budgets by an annual average of 2% of GDP to absorb the revenue shock. In 2018, debt rose to the equivalent of 38.2% of GDP, partly to finance extra expenditure needs but mostly because of debt revaluation including arrears for SOE debt guarantees. The impact of disasters on economic activity, along with the need to spend for post-disaster response, has prevented PNG from meeting targets under its medium-term fiscal strategies for 2013–2017 and 2018–2022; the country appears unlikely to limit its fiscal deficit to the equivalent of 1% of GDP and debt at 30% of GDP by 2022.

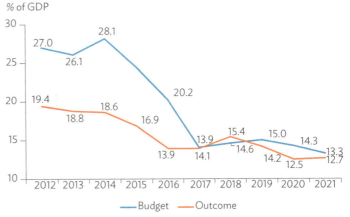

Figure 10: Papua New Guinea Revenue: Budget versus Outcome

GDP = gross domestic product.
Sources: Government of Papua New Guinea national budget reports.

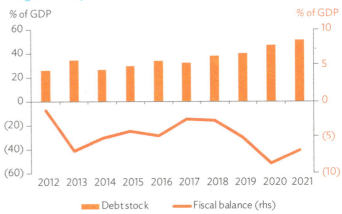

Figure 11: Papua New Guinea Fiscal Balance and Debt Stock

( ) = negative, GDP = gross domestic product, rhs = right-hand scale.
Sources: Government of Papua New Guinea national budget reports.

OPERATIONALIZING PNG'S COMMITMENT TO ADDRESS CLIMATE CHANGE

PNG is a member of the Vulnerable Twenty (V20) group and ranks 149th out of 181 countries in terms of its vulnerability to, and readiness for, climate change challenges (Global Carbon Atlas). The country has made some effort to review and enact legislative and policy frameworks to address the effects of climate change and help PNG meet its commitments under international conventions and treaties, including the Sendai Framework for Disaster Reduction and Strategic Program for Climate Resilience. PNG was also the first country to formally submit the final version of its NDC under the Paris Climate Agreement and has localized four Sustainable Development Goals indicators on climate change to be implemented over 2015–2030.

However, progress in addressing climate change issues, including in incorporating climate and disaster risk into sector plans and funded programs, has been slow. PNG also lags in ensuring that climate resilience engineering designs are mainstreamed into civil infrastructures, building

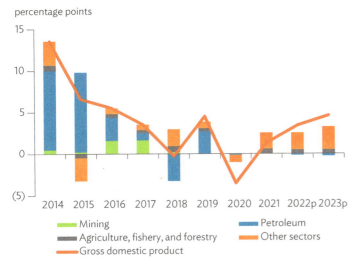

Figure 9: Papua New Guinea Contributions to Gross Domestic Product Growth in Real Terms

( ) = negative, p = projection.
Source: Government of Papua New Guinea National Statistical Office.

codes, and sector operations, except for development aid projects. Lack of data makes it challenging for forward planning and projections for the reduction of greenhouse gas emissions.

Further, weak policies and institutional frameworks limit the government's ability to provide timely responses to affected communities in the wake of a disaster. As a result, most assistance has been provided by development partners in the past. PNG's macroeconomic policy framework also has not been accommodative of shocks, with resources being diverted from essential services to cover relief cost. For example, following the 2015 drought, the government instructed the district development authorities to use K2 million of their District Service Improvement Program allocations for relief assistance (RNZ 2015a). Capital investment budgets were slashed, which has serious implications on medium-term growth. Fiscal deficit and debt exceeded planned targets, increasing the country's vulnerability to debt distress.

In response to these concerns, ADB is working to help PNG build resilience to economic- and disaster-related shocks and mitigate the impacts of climate change. It supports selected disaster resilience programs in line with PNG's National Disaster Risk Reduction Framework by assessing structural vulnerability, reviewing technical specifications for road design, and bolstering national mechanisms to screen investments and programs against disaster risk and assess their contribution to long-term climate change adaptation. Besides ensuring that environmental sustainability is mainstreamed in all its operations, ADB's support for the energy sector through the Power Sector Development Project is aligned with PNG's NDC.

The government may also wish to consider investing in alternate climate- and disaster-resilient transport infrastructures surrounding key economic project areas, investments to reduce the dependency of the Ok Tedi mine on the Fly River for shipment and thus safeguard the mine's operations during droughts. The government plans to further explore disaster risk financing and insurance solutions, as well as preventive budget planning options to increase PNG's financial resilience, in coordination with development partners.

PNG can also tap less-costly climate financing as a way of easing the fiscal burden of resilient infrastructure investments. ADB's Strategic Climate Fund and Climate Change cofinancing options are available to support the government's climate change mitigation and adaptation objectives. The Strategic Climate Fund is funding a joint project between ADB and the Government of Australia to upgrade the 60-year-old wharf in Alotau, Milne Bay Province. The upgrade includes climate-proofing features that will enable the wharf to withstand climate shocks and sea-level rise.

Strengthening public financial management is also key to securing adequate resources to respond to shocks and mitigate risks from climate change and disasters. ADB is working with the government to improve fiscal and debt management by providing technical assistance to address capacity constraints and institutional weaknesses in macro-fiscal management, and supporting the strengthening of SOEs' institutional and governance arrangements. Further, it is important that PNG mainstream climate change issues into its sectoral, including macroeconomic, policies. This way, risks are accounted for and relevant policies and plans adequately resourced, including budgeting for capital investment to support climate-resilient growth.

CONCLUSION

PNG is highly vulnerable to climatic and disaster shocks that are expected to become more frequent and severe with climate change. The adverse impact of the shocks can threaten lives, cut off the country's economic lifeline, and stress the government's finances. These shocks have reduced export earnings and economic growth, which, in turn, have lowered government revenue and increased fiscal deficits and public debt to above government targets.

The country can build resilience to economic- and disaster-related shocks and mitigate the impacts of climate change by mainstreaming climate change in sector-wide policies and plans, including fiscal policy and the national budget framework. PNG can tap available, less costly climate financing to ease the fiscal burden of investing in building resilient infrastructure. Finally, strengthening public financial management, for instance through building macro-fiscal management capacity and pursuing SOE reforms, is also key to securing adequate resources for disaster response and climate change adaptation. Combined, these measures would help PNG become more resilient to climatic risks and disaster shocks when they arise.

References

Allen, B. J. and R. M. Bourke. 2001. The 1997 Drought and Frost in PNG: Overview and Policy Implications. In Bourke, R. M., M.G. Allen, and J.G. Salisbury, eds. *Food Security for Papua New Guinea*. Canberra: Australian Centre for International Agricultural Research.

Asian Development Bank (ADB). *Asian Development Outlook (ADO) Series*. (accessed 22 June 2022).

ADB. 1998. *Asian Development Outlook 1998: Population and Human Resources*. Manila.

ADB. 2020. *Country Partnership Strategy: Papua New Guinea, 2021–2025—Achieving Diversified, Sustained, and Inclusive Growth*. Manila.

ADB. 2022. *Report and Recommendation of the President to the Board of Directors: Proposed Loans to Papua New Guinea for the Power Sector Development Project*. Manila.

Extractives Industries Transparency Initiative. 2019. *EITI Progress Report 2019*.

Global Carbon Atlas. CO_2 *Emissions*.

Government of Papua New Guinea, Bank of Papua New Guinea. 2021. *Annual Reports and Financial Statements 31 December 2019*. Port Moresby.

Government of Papua New Guinea National Statistical Office. 2021. *Papua New Guinea National Accounts 2013–2019*. Port Moresby.

Radio New Zealand (RNZ). 2015a. PNG govt announces drought relief funds process. 23 October.

RNZ. 2015b. Porgera mine back up and running after drought closure. 23 November.

United Nations. 1992. *United Nations Framework Convention on Climate Change.*

United Nations. 1998. *Kyoto Protocol to the United Nations Framework Convention on Climate Change.*

United Nations. 2009. *Report of the Conference of the Parties on its fifteenth session, held in Copenhagen from 7 to 19 December 2009.*

United Nations. 2015. *Paris Agreement.*

Promoting climate and fiscal resiliency in Solomon Islands

Lead authors: Jacqueline Connell and Prince Cruz

Solomon Islands faces fiscal challenges that are compounded by its exposure to climate change and disasters from natural hazards. The COVID-19 pandemic and the social unrest in the capital, Honiara, in 2021 have increased the immediate fiscal pressures. In the longer-term, Solomon Islands faces rising development spending needs for its fast-growing population, while a decline in logging will lower government revenues. Investment in climate-resilient infrastructure, and maintenance to preserve it, will add to the spending needs. This article lays out how the government is responding to these fiscal challenges and what additional steps could be taken. Accessing concessional financing is part of the response. Another is tax reform to mobilize more stable domestic revenue. Equally important will be incorporating climate mitigation and adaptation plans into medium-term budgeting.

Solomon Islands' population, which mostly reside in coastal areas, is exposed to extreme rainfall events, tropical cyclones, earthquakes, and sea-level rise. The country's disaster risk is the second highest in the world, according to the WorldRiskReport 2021. The scattered geography, consisting of many islands, contributes to large infrastructure gaps and adaptation needs. Only about 16% of the population are connected to the electricity grid, and nearly all grid-connected power is generated by diesel (Figure 12 and ADB 2021).

Given these challenges, investments in climate-resilient infrastructures can have long-term benefits. Analysis by the IMF suggests that prioritizing climate-proofing capital investment can lessen the negative impact of disasters on Solomon Islands' growth, fiscal balances, and debt sustainability (IMF 2022a). If well-targeted, climate investments could also stimulate private sector investment, helping to support economic growth.

Despite these benefits, there is limited fiscal space for the government to invest in climate-resilient infrastructure. The economy is forecast to contract for the third consecutive year in 2022. Even before the pandemic, growth had slowed, and domestic revenues had fallen from 30.5% of GDP in 2017 to 25.6% in 2019 of GDP (Figure 13). Economic contraction during 2020 and 2021 contributed to revenue falling further to 24.2% of GDP in 2021. A decline in logging contributed to the weak revenue. Export duties on logging almost halved from 6.1% of GDP in 2018 to an estimated 3.2% in 2021.

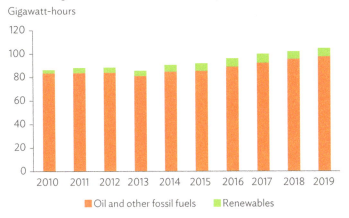

Figure 12: Solomon Islands Energy Generation

Renewables generate less than 10% of electricity.

Source: International Renewable Energy Agency. 2021. Renewable energy statistics 2021.

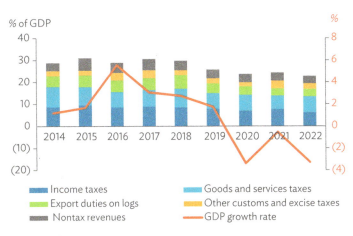

Figure 13: Solomon Islands Domestic Revenues and GDP Growth

Revenues have trended down since 2017, driven partly by lower logging revenue.

( ) = negative, GDP = gross domestic product.
Sources: Solomon Islands National Statistics Office, Ministry of Finance and Treasury budget documents, and ADB estimates.

Although the fiscal deficit was contained at 3.8% of GDP in 2021, fiscal pressures are expected to mount in 2022 because of multiple shocks (Figure 14). The government planned a fiscal deficit of 7.6% of GDP in its 2022 budget, to be financed mainly through grants and external borrowing. The 2022 budget includes supportive measures such as a 50% duty exemption on fuel imports for 6 months, and allocations for a community transmission response, a civil unrest rehabilitation response, and economic recovery support.

Figure 14: Solomon Islands Fiscal Balance

Fiscal deficit widened in 2020 and 2021 as revenues fell.

( ) = negative, GDP = gross domestic product.
Sources: Ministry of Finance and Treasury budget documents, and ADB estimates.

Given the limited fiscal space, accessing climate financing will help ensure sufficient investments in adaptation and mitigation. Although almost all climate adaptation projects in the Pacific have been financed through grants, Solomon Islands has also received concessional loans (IMF 2021). Public debt was estimated equal to 15.3% in 2021, but is expected to rise over the medium term to finance infrastructure investments and fiscal deficits (Figure 15).

Solomon Islands was able to tap around $112 million in climate change and disaster risk financing from 2010 to 2016, according to an assessment published by the Pacific Community (SPC 2017). Although this was a substantial amount relative to the funding available, the overall impact of these projects was assessed as "very minimal considering the scattered nature of Solomon Islands communities and provinces."

Figure 15: Solomon Islands Public Debt

Public debt has risen since 2016 from a low level.

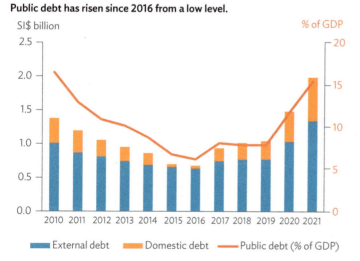

GDP = gross domestic product.
Source: ADB estimates using data from Ministry of Finance and Treasury.

To increase the prospect of accessing climate financing, the government established a Climate Finance Resilience Unit in the Ministry of Finance and Treasury in 2021. The unit is intended to help Solomon Islands achieve accreditation for climate financing (Pacific Islands Forum 2022).

Another way to improve climate and fiscal resilience is to strengthen domestic revenue mobilization. Taxes from logging, which account for about 22% of total tax revenue, are exposed to international demand and price fluctuations, and are likely to decline over the medium-term due to diminished resources (Government of Solomon Islands 2021). Meanwhile, the broader tax system of Solomon Islands is complex, expensive to administer, and relies on high rates applied to a narrow base, which discourages compliance.

The government commenced a review of its tax framework in 2017 to look at ways to mobilize revenue in a more efficient manner. A Tax Administration Bill was submitted to Parliament in May 2022, which aims to modernize and unify the administration of all tax types. There are plans to introduce a value-added tax to replace various goods taxes, sales tax, stamp duties, and customs duties that have multiple rates of tax, and different rules and procedures.

Broadening the tax base and modernizing tax administration could help achieve a more sustainable revenue base to fund climate-resilient infrastructure and other public services.

As the economy recovers from the contraction caused by the COVID-19 pandemic, the government can also start to build its fiscal buffers to manage climate shocks. Solomon Islands has not established a disaster fund that it can draw on for immediate liquidity after a shock. Instead, it mainly relies on cash reserves, contingency warrants, and development partner support.

In 2021, the government's cash balance had fallen to less than one month of recurrent spending (IMF 2022b). To finance unforeseen expenditure, including on disasters, the 2022 budget provides for SI$20.0 million ($2.5 million) in contingent warrants (about 0.5% of planned government expenditure). The government also has access to contingent financing after a disaster or health crisis from ADB's Pacific Disaster Resilience Program (a contingent disaster financing instrument). Solomon Islands accessed $5 million following the COVID-19 community transmission in early 2022.

Aside from mobilizing resources and building fiscal buffers, continued efforts are needed to improve the efficiency of public investment management. Because adaptation needs are large and resources are limited, there is a need for effective project appraisal and selection to ensure that projects with the highest social returns are selected.

Another crucial step is to integrate adaptation and mitigation plans into the government budget. Although development partners are financing much of the construction costs associated with new climate-resilient infrastructure, these assets will require maintenance which will add to the government's recurrent expenditure. Introducing a climate expenditure tagging system to the chart of accounts could enable climate-related expenditure to be easily monitored in the budget. Over time, this could help to identify financing gaps, galvanize additional investment, and improve the accountability of climate financing activities.

References

ADB. 2021. *Pacific Energy Update 2021*. Manila.

Government of Solomon Islands. 2021. *2021 Nationally Determined Contributions*. Honiara.

Government of Solomon Islands. 2022. *2022 Financial Policy, Objectives, and Strategies, Budget Paper: Volume 1*. Honiara.

International Monetary Fund (IMF). 2021a. *Unlocking Access to Climate Finance for Pacific Island Countries*. Washington, DC.

IMF. 2022a. *Solomon Islands: Selected Issues – Spending Needs for Achieving SDGs with Climate Resilience*. Washington, DC.

IMF. 2022b. Solomon Islands 2021 Article IV Consultation. *IMF Country Report No. 22/14*. Washington, DC.

The Pacific Community (SPC). 2017. *Solomon Islands Climate Change and Disaster Risk Finance Assessment – Final Report*. Suva.

Pacific Islands Forum. 2022. RELEASE: Enhancing climate resilience financing in the Solomon Islands.

South Pacific economies: Counting the costs, preparing for the future

Lead author: James Webb

COVID-19, measles outbreaks, cyclones, and the Hunga-Tonga Hunga-Ha'apai (HTHH) eruption have shown how vulnerable South Pacific economies (SPEs; being the Cook Islands, Niue, Samoa, and Tonga) are to sudden disasters and economic shocks. These shocks can have lasting impacts on economic development and fiscal balances. For COVID-19, the direct economic impact for the SPEs was largely in the private sector, especially tourism, but fiscal balances have also been dramatically weakened. In this context, this article seeks to outline the impacts of COVID-19 and the HTHH eruption on SPEs' ability to manage future economic shocks, including disasters. While a degraded debt position and vulnerable tourism industry in the Cook Islands will likely recover in the absence of another major economic shock, the grant resources that have been made available to Tonga, Samoa, and Niue have mitigated the fiscal and economic damage of the pandemic, supporting future disaster resilience.

INCREASINGLY VULNERABLE ECONOMIES

The South Pacific is no stranger to significant disasters that are triggered by natural hazards. For example, Cyclone Evan, which hit Samoa in 2012, resulted in damages and losses equivalent to an estimated 28% of GDP. Destroyed physical assets represented an estimated 109% of the normal value of construction activities in Samoa, inferring that recovery and reconstruction would take between 2 and 3 years.[1] Of these damaged assets, 55% were owned by the public sector and the balance held by private enterprises and individuals. Total financing needs were estimated at $206 million. GDP declined by 4.1% in fiscal year (FY) 2012 (FY2012, ended on 30 June 2012 for all SPEs) and fell a further 2.3% in FY2013. However, strong GDP growth of 6.8% in FY2014 (fueled partly by reconstruction projects) brought total economic activity back above the pre-cyclone level by the end of that fiscal year, just 2 years after the cyclone (Figure 16).

In Niue, the economy sustained significant damage to infrastructure and agriculture in 2004 because of Cyclone Heta. The category 5 cyclone cost the small island economy more than $60 million in damage and economic losses, almost 6 times the value of GDP in FY2003. GDP declined by 3.7% in FY2004 before climbing by 8.9% in FY2005 because of the reconstruction program, returning GDP to above the pre-crisis level by the end of the year.

Economic shocks beyond natural hazards have also caused significant contractions in previous periods. In Tonga, the 2006 Nuku'alofa riots destroyed 80% of the central business district and resulted in a large public sector pay settlement.[2] The disruption to economic activity and the fall in both public and private investments following the riots led the GDP to decline by 4.6% in FY2007. The Tongan economy returned to its FY2006 level by FY2009 and was comfortably above pre-crisis levels in the following year.

The impact on the global financial crisis in the Cook Islands caused declines in various sectors of the economy, led by tourism. Visitor arrivals in the Cook Islands decreased by 2.6% in FY2008, as global travel began to slow. This contributed to a cumulative 5.2% fall in GDP across 2 fiscal years. After a brief period of volatility, strong growth of 4.0% in FY2012 saw activity return to near pre-crisis levels, but the economy had not completely recovered from the initial shock until a full 6 years after the initial recession.

Figure 16: GDP Levels Relative to Economic Shocks

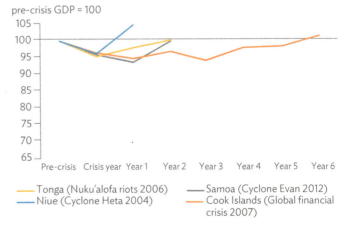

GDP = gross domestic product.
Source: Asian Development Outlook database and estimates.

The COVID-19 pandemic is a larger, longer-lasting, and more complex shock than any that the Pacific has felt before. Rather than a relatively short period of economic disruption from previous crises, the direct economic impacts of COVID-19 have been a multiyear degradation of public health and private sector activity, especially in the tourism sector. Consequently, this has dramatically affected fiscal balances through reduced tax revenues and increased health and stimulus spending. Further, disruptions to supply chains and mobilization of technical staff have delayed major capital works and private sector construction, another pillar of economic activity.

Tourism has been the major casualty of the pandemic with serious fallout for SPEs. According to the South Pacific Tourism Organisation, tourism receipts were equivalent to 66.0% of GDP in the Cook Islands, 28.0% of GDP in Niue, 24.5% of GDP in Samoa, and 11.0% in Tonga in FY2019. A 2-year shutdown of tourism activity has had unprecedented economic implications.

As compared to FY2019, it is estimated that GDP in FY2022 is 3.5% lower in Tonga,[3] 10.1% lower in Samoa, and 26.7% lower in the Cook Islands (Figure 17).

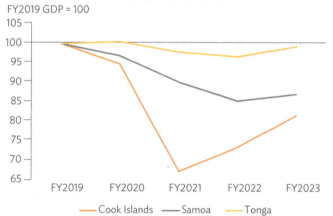

Figure 17: South Pacific Economies GDP Relative to Before COVID-19

COVID-19 = coronavirus disease, FY = fiscal year, GDP = gross domestic product.
Note: FY2019 ended on 30 June 2019.
Source: Asian Development Outlook database and estimates.

For Samoa and the Cook Islands, these contractions have been focused almost entirely in the private sector because of the importance of tourism and related services. Of a cumulative decline of 10.0% in GDP in Samoa between FY2019 and FY2021, the services sector contributed 5.6 percentage points and the industry sector contributed a further 2.6 percentage points; in the Cook Islands, the services sector contributed 23.4 percentage points to the 32.8% decline in overall GDP and industry an additional 4.3 percentage points. In both cases, tourism and construction were the major drivers, with public capital spending and public employment relatively constant despite large increases in other areas of recurrent government spending to mitigate the impacts of COVID-19.

In the case of Tonga, the HTHH eruption and subsequent tsunami further highlighted the ongoing exposure of SPEs to disasters. While initially less affected by the economic impacts of COVID-19 than its South Pacific peers, the eruption and tsunami caused combined damages and economic losses estimated at 36.4% of GDP.[4] The FY2023 Tongan budget estimates that this will require reconstruction costs of $248.6 million spread over at least 3 years. However, even prior to the eruption, the 2.2% decline in GDP in FY2021 relative to FY2019 was driven by a 4.2 percentage point decline in the services sector, almost all of which was tourism-related.

The impact of the last 2 years on the private sector is unprecedented, and it is unclear how this will affect the long-term recovery prospects for the South Pacific region. Government interventions appear to have mitigated widespread business closures, but with dramatic declines in tourism activity, labor has migrated to other industries or offshore. Prior to the pandemic, tourism employed an estimated 40% of the workforce in Niue in FY2019, 34% in the Cook Islands, 15% in Samoa, and 9% in Tonga.[5] In preparing for the recovery, country consultations with industry bodies suggest that labor shortages exist in key positions such as chefs, managers, and other specialized staff who have found jobs elsewhere or could not be retained otherwise. A similar impact has been observed in retaining engineers and builders, many of whom have likely moved to Australia and New Zealand, where pay rates are higher and labor in the construction industry is also scarce.

Many hoteliers also require significant reinvestment to bring facilities back online. However, corporate balance sheets are likely to be significantly degraded because of the extended period of diminished economic activity, limiting the ability to undertake refurbishment and reinvestment programs, recruit new staff, and replenish inventories. Financial support or credit may be required. Repayment holidays and cautious lending practices may have shielded financial markets from rising nonperforming loans, but cautious lending at this stage of the recovery has kept business credit growth relatively low, especially in the services sectors.

Even if travelers return in significant numbers, as early trends in Fiji and the Cook Islands suggest, the recovery will likely be uneven and some businesses may not survive despite making it through the worst of the crisis. This is a particular risk for Samoa, Tonga, and Niue, as not only do they face supply-side issues associated with border closures (and reconstruction in Tonga), but delayed reopening may affect their ability to reclaim their share of regional travelers. Although trends indicate steady recovery in the important source markets of Australia and New Zealand, with a higher share of travelers choosing the Pacific rather than longer haul routes to other destinations, these have yet to fully recover to pre-COVID-19 pandemic levels. In April 2022, Australian outbound residents reached 39.4% of their April 2019 levels, whereas for New Zealand outbound travelers in June 2022 reached 42.5% of their June 2019 levels.

Mitigating this impact in Samoa and Tonga has been the dramatic rise in household income and consumption driven by increased remittances. This, together with development partner grants, more than fully offset the lost income from tourism in Tonga. Compared to the same periods in 2019, remittances in Samoa were 19.7% higher in the 12 months to April 2022 and 43.1% higher in the 12 months to December 2021 in Tonga. Remittances reached a record 35.3% of GDP in Samoa and 46.6% in Tonga in FY2021. These are well above pre-pandemic levels, and ADB estimates that remittances will fall in coming years.

Taken together, this raises the prospect of smaller, more vulnerable private sectors across SPEs, with less financial and organizational capacity to weather future disasters. The recovery in tourism is also far from guaranteed, with the global industry still in the early stages of recovery and SPEs facing numerous challenges in tourism growth even prior to the pandemic (PSDI 2021a). Governments have all recognized the ongoing need to stimulate economic activity and signaled their intent to embark on major capital expansions, supplementing the private sector recovery and continuing to stress fiscal balances.

ARE FISCAL POSITIONS UP TO THE TASK?

The frequent and severe impacts of disasters and economic shocks on fiscal resources have prompted national governments and development partners to improve the planning and provision of contingent financing.

Samoa, Tonga, and the Cook Islands are all members of the Pacific Catastrophic Risk Insurance Corporation (PCRIC). However, since its establishment, only two payouts have been made: to Tonga for the 2018 Cyclone Gita ($3.5 million) and 2020 Cyclone Harold ($4.5 million). Importantly, PCRIC policies are driven by asset damage valuations within the disaster area and not meant to cover ongoing economic and fiscal needs.

SPEs have other financial arrangements in place for emergency response, including annual contingencies or emergency funds within existing budgets. However, in the event of a significant disaster, emergency funds are typically insufficient to meet all in-year financing needs. Transfers between budget lines (i.e., virements) typically face restrictions without some form of parliamentary approval. Governments have thus used their own disaster response funds for immediate response and relied more heavily on amending budget appropriations. Supplementary budgets, which can appropriate larger sums but take time to secure, often redirect funds from development priorities and require parliamentary approval. Without external support or excess revenues, the central budget bears the full cost through the drawdown of government reserves, reducing other areas of spending, or increased debt.

Prior to the advent of COVID-19, SPEs had made significant headway in improving fiscal resilience. General fiscal discipline, an avoidance of non-concessional debt financing, and enhanced revenue collection led to improved debt positions. At the same time, Tonga and Samoa's debt distress ratings were raised from *moderate* to *high* risk in 2017 by the IMF because of the inclusion of disaster risk into its debt modelling, enabling multilateral institutions like ADB and the World Bank to offer development finance on grant terms (rather than concessional loans) and reducing the need for debt financing.

In Samoa, from a fiscal deficit of 5.3% of GDP in FY2014—largely caused by financing Cyclone Evan reconstruction—expenditure controls and growing revenues led to a fiscal surplus of 2.8% of GDP by FY2019. Domestic revenue mobilization saw continued improvements in tax collection, which, as a percentage of GDP, increased from 22.1% in FY2015 to 26.7% in FY2020, just before the private sector felt the full impact of the pandemic. The public debt-to-GDP ratio trended downward during the same period, falling from a high of 58.9% in FY2015 to 47.6% in FY2020—below the authorities' ceiling of 50.0% of GDP.

In Tonga, tax policy reforms and improved tax administration helped raise the tax-to-GDP ratio from 15.9% in FY2012 to 20.6% in FY2020 despite economic setbacks from a series of cyclones. Overall, domestic revenues increased from the equivalent of 18.0% of GDP in FY2012 to 24.3% in FY2020. However, these fell in FY2021 as the COVID-19 impacted trade, tourism, and local businesses. Similar to Samoa, Tonga's external debt declined from 45.3% of GDP in FY2013 to an estimated 39.6% in FY2021, with both countries able to meet most of their additional financing needs via grant resources.

In the Cook Islands, recurrent spending declined from the equivalent of 31.8% of GDP in FY2012 to 28.2% in FY2019. Following successful tax reforms from 2013, total revenue increased from 36.4% of GDP in FY2016 to 42.3% in FY2019. The successive years of fiscal surplus since FY2016 (averaging 4.6% of GDP) enabled the creation of a stabilization account, equivalent to 11.4% of FY2019 GDP, to guard against economic and fiscal shocks; and the loan reserve fund, a sinking fund equivalent to 4.3% of FY2019 GDP, to smooth debt servicing requirements. Debt financing, which has been low and stable and used predominantly for infrastructure investment, fell from a peak of 26.4% of GDP in FY2016 to 17.1% of GDP in FY2020 after accounting for prepayments.

SPE governments recognized that a large fiscal response was needed to mitigate the economic fallout of closed borders with dramatic increases in social protection grants, support payments to households, business support measures, and increased health spending. This resulted in large funding requirements across all SPEs. At the same time, tax revenue fell rapidly. By FY2021, tax revenue had fallen by 5.4% in Samoa, and current expenditures had risen by 14.0%, relative to FY2019. Similarly in Tonga, tax revenues fell by 6.7% and current spending had increased by 18.6%. The tourism-dependent Cook Islands was by far the hardest hit, with a 45.6% fall in tax receipts in FY2021 relative to FY2019 and a 51.5% increase in current spending, driven by an historic economic stimulus package spread across 2 years.

Smaller than expected declines in tax revenue, increases in non-tax revenues, as well as sizeable budget support from development partners, led to fiscal surpluses or small deficits in Samoa and Tonga from FY2020 through to FY2022 (Figure 18).[6] Debt has remained unchanged or fallen in nominal terms, setting a solid foundation for maintaining their resilience to future disaster events. In the Cook Islands, however, the fiscal gap over this period has been financed through the complete drawdown of accumulated reserves, additional grant funding from New Zealand, and loans from ADB and the Asian Infrastructure Investment Bank. Because of the mixture of grants and loans, Cook Islands debt increased from 16.7% of GDP in FY2019 to 43.5% in FY2022. This compares to an estimated debt-to-GDP ratio in FY2022 of 37.8% in Tonga and 47.4% in Samoa—near their pre-crisis levels. Niue continues to adhere to its policy of no debt financing, with New Zealand providing budget support grants to compensate for declining tax revenue and increased expenditures.

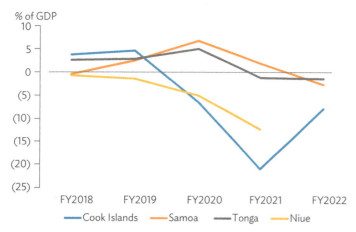

Figure 18: South Pacific Economies Fiscal Balances

( ) = negative, FY = fiscal year, GDP = gross domestic product.
Note: FY2019 ended on 30 June 2019.
Source: ADB estimates.

In the case of Samoa, Tonga, and Niue, the rapid mobilization of budget support grants and contingent financing has ensured fiscal resilience through the COVID-19 crisis and preserved fiscal space for the next economic shock. None of these countries required significant new loans to meet the rapid escalation in external financing needs, so debt levels have continued to fall.

For the Cook Islands, limited access to additional development partner grants required it to draw down its large cash reserves and reverse its comfortable debt position prior to COVID-19. With tourism representing up to 66% of its pre-pandemic GDP, the fallout of the 2-year tourism shutdown posed an existential threat to its previously booming tourism economy, which took decades to develop. By acting quickly to mobilize concessional financing, the Cook Islands mitigated a possible collapse of the tourism industry and avoided a government solvency crisis which could have damaged the economy for generations—potentially far worse than the economic collapse in 1996 which dramatically escalated out-migration. With high vaccination rates and open borders since January 2022, the retention of a large portion of domestic tourism operators could help the Cook Islands be one of the quickest South Pacific economies to recover from the economic impacts of the pandemic. Recognizing the importance of sustaining the economic recovery and supporting the government cash position, the government and ADB have agreed to a Precautionary Financing Option of $40 million which would back-stop the government's fiscal position if the recovery falters, buying the private sector more time if needed.

CONCLUSION

The SPEs have done remarkably well in strengthening revenue collection, with high tax collection rates relative to their peers. Previous reforms improved public financial positions and enabled them to withstand recent economic shocks, such as the COVID-19 pandemic and the HTHH eruption. Moreover, contingent financing products from the World Bank and ADB have clearly played a key role in addressing the fiscal needs of South Pacific governments alongside rapid grant support from Australia and New Zealand. With economic recovery still underway, these partners will continue to play an outsized role in ensuring fiscal and economic resilience both now and into the future.

However, the impacts of recent shocks have been severe and persistent. The bigger issue will be the pace of economic recovery and whether it can support government revenues enough to meet spending needs. Growing own-source revenues will be central to supporting fiscal sustainability, restoring fiscal buffers, and reestablishing a strong foundation for the next potential crisis. Governments will need to finely balance their expenditure priorities—especially in the Cook Islands, where fiscal buffers have been significantly eroded, and Tonga, where an impending increase in debt servicing costs in FY2024 will need provisioning and reconstruction needs remain. Large reductions in expenditure may further damage a vulnerable private sector recovery, but improving the quality of spending programs should remain a key focus alongside further revenue reforms and improved compliance.

Structural reforms, e.g., multi-hazard early warning systems and contingent financing products from multilateral development banks, have often occurred in the wake of repeated disasters, and experiences during the COVID-19 pandemic will likely support changes in public health delivery and pandemic management. Time will tell whether more serious structural fiscal or economic adjustments are required, especially if government revenues can no longer support elevated levels of spending because of sustained damage to the private sector. The nascent economic recovery remains at risk, and the HTHH eruption should serve as a warning that the South Pacific not only needs to recover from the current crisis but also position itself to weather potential future shocks.

Endnotes

[1] World Bank. 2013. *Samoa Post-Disaster Needs Assessment Cyclone Evan 2012*. Washington, DC.

[2] World Bank. 2008. *Tonga: Trade Brief*. Washington, DC.

[3] Although this includes the impact of the HTHH eruption and subsequent tsunami.

4. Initial Damage Assessment by the World Bank and the Global Facility for Disaster Reduction and Recovery (Global Rapid Post-Disaster Rapid Estimation).

5. South Pacific Tourism Organisation, as cited in the ADB Private Sector Development Initiative (2021b) Tourism snapshots.

6. This does not suggest, however, that all financing needs have been met. Notably, damages in Tonga may take years to be fully addressed, and expenditure may not occur in the year that grants revenue is received.

References

ADB. *Asian Development Outlook (ADO) Series.* (accessed 13 July 2022).

Pacific Private Sector Development Initiative (PSDI). 2021a. *Looking Forward Vol. 1: Evaluating the Challenges for Pacific Tourism after COVID-19.* Sydney.

PSDI. 2021b. *Tourism snapshots.* Sydney.

World Bank. 2008. *Tonga: Trade Brief.* Washington, DC.

World Bank. 2013. *Samoa Post-Disaster Needs Assessment Cyclone Evan 2012.* Washington, DC.

The challenge of financing a climate emergency for Vanuatu

Lead authors: Jacqueline Connell and Prince Cruz

In May 2022, the Government of Vanuatu declared a climate emergency, highlighting the country's vulnerability to extreme weather events. Vanuatu is taking steps to reduce the adverse impact of climate change and disasters caused by natural hazards on its economy, including by investing in climate resilient infrastructure. The large cost associated with adaptation, mitigation, and damages from disasters means that accessing concessional resources, and mobilizing domestic revenue, will be crucial to meet the rising development spending needs. Equally important will be the ongoing efforts to improve public investment management and build fiscal reserves to buffer against climate-induced shocks.

Adding together the cumulative cost of adaptation, mitigation and recovery for damages and losses from disasters, the government estimates that the "real cost" of achieving Vanuatu's NDC under the Paris Agreement will reach $1.2 billion by 2030. Although expected to be spread over several years, this cost is about 120% of 2021 GDP. Around 60% of the cost is for adaptation, 26% for mitigation, and the remainder for recovery of losses and damages (Government of Vanuatu 2022).

In its declaration of a climate emergency, the government identified climate change as the "single biggest threat" to the livelihood, security, and well-being of Vanuatu's people. The declaration served to (i) put the government on record in support of taking emergency actions; and (ii) elevate the climate change related human rights campaign at the upcoming United Nation General Assembly in September (Government of Vanuatu 2022).

Vanuatu's disaster risk is the highest in the world, according to the WorldRiskReport 2021. Aside from cyclones, Vanuatu is at risk of volcanic eruptions, earthquakes, tsunamis, and climate-induced events, such as sea-level rise. In the past, disasters have had an outsized impact on Vanuatu's economy. Damage caused by Cyclone Harold, which struck in 2020, was estimated to be equivalent to more than 50% of GDP (Government of Vanuatu 2020).

The frequency and severity of disasters also affect Vanuatu's fiscal and debt sustainability (World Bank 2021). Damage to properties and livelihoods erode the economic base for revenue collection. Meanwhile, reconstruction and upgrading of infrastructure adds to expenditure, and can increase borrowing. For example, disbursements for reconstruction and upgrading of infrastructure following Cyclone Pam in 2015, contributed to an increase in public debt from the equivalent of 23% of GDP in 2014 to 45% in 2017 (ADB 2018).

Vanuatu has taken steps to climate-proof infrastructure such as roads, bridges, water catchment, and buildings under several initiatives such as the Vanuatu Coastal Adaptation Project. Although climate-proofing infrastructure may be more expensive initially, it can yield high returns in the long-run by reducing economic disruption and disaster recovery costs (IMF 2021). For instance, a climate-proofed airport should be able to withstand category 5 cyclones and can immediately be used for relief operations after a storm has passed. It can also enable a tourism recovery to begin sooner. Cyclone Pam (which affected 188,000 people in 2015) and Cyclone Harold (83,837 people in 2020) were both category 5 cyclones.

Likewise, the transition to renewable energy involves heavy capital costs but yields substantial savings in operating costs. About 24.4% of Vanuatu's electricity was generated from renewable sources in 2019 (Figure 19).

Government plans for expansion of electricity access involve a large increase in generation using renewables. Vanuatu's NDC approved in 2019 targets 50% energy generation from renewable sources by 2025, with the target rising to 100% by 2030 (Government of Vanuatu 2019). This increase is proposed to be driven by a rising use of solar, wind, and geothermal power and coconut oil from 2019 levels (Figure 20).

Figure 19: Vanuatu Energy Generation Mix

Despite increase in share of renewables, more than 75% of energy generated in 2019 was from diesel.

Source: Government of Vanuatu. 2019. *NDC Implementation Roadmap*. Port Vila; and United Nations Development Program. 2020. *Enhancing and Fast-tracking Implementation of Vanuatu's Nationally Determined Contribution (NDC)*. Port Vila.

Figure 20: Vanuatu Renewable Energy Generation, 2019

Hydropower and solar are the main sources of renewable energy.

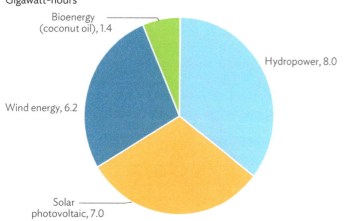

Source: International Renewable Energy Agency. 2021. Renewable energy statistics 2021.

Mobilizing resources to make the economy more climate- and disaster-resilient is a medium- to long-term agenda that is likely to involve several strategies. In the short term, the government faces fiscal pressure from increased spending needs in the aftermath of the COVID-19 community transmission.

In its 2022 budget, the government planned a deficit of 5.1% of GDP, following a fiscal surplus of 2.6% of GDP in 2021 (Figure 21). Budgeted expenditure is projected to increase by 17.4%, compared with the 2021 estimated expenditure, while revenues remain about the same. The 2022 budget includes a 20.6% increase in capital spending, which includes allocations for making airports more climate-resilient. In response to domestic transmission of COVID-19, a Vt1.2 billion ($10.6 million) supplementary budget was passed in May, raising total expenditure by 2.4%. Of this, Vt200 million ($1.8 million) would replenish the emergency fund.

Figure 21: Vanuatu Fiscal Balance

Fiscal balance turned to a deficit in 2020 before returning to a surplus in 2021.

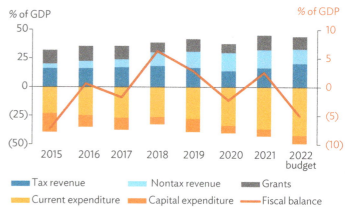

( ) = negative, GDP = gross domestic product.
Source: ADB estimates using data from budget documents.

Revenues from the Honorary Citizenship Programs (HCPs), which provide passports in exchange for investment, have helped shore up the fiscal balance, though their long-term contribution is uncertain. Revised to its current form in 2015 to finance reconstruction following Cyclone Pam, HCPs, contribution to revenue and grants reached 36.3% in 2020, but declined to 29.0% in 2021. The government has used windfall HCPs revenue, which has exceeded budget estimates, to build cash reserves, finance spending on disasters, and pay down debt.

After rising by an average of 47.5% yearly from 2017 to 2020, HCPs revenue dropped by 10.5% in 2021. The loss of a correspondent banking relationship and concerns on the due diligence prior to the issuance of passports may have contributed to this decline. In March 2022, the Council of the European Union suspended its visa waiver agreement for Vanuatu passports issued after May 2015, which could reduce demand for honorary passports further.

The government is exploring options to mobilize more domestic revenue. In 2021, it appointed the National Revenue Governance Committee to develop policy options to broaden the revenue base. Raising additional revenue, however, is challenging with the relatively small economic base, and less than 20% of the working-age population in formal employment, according to the 2020 census. The IMF (2021) estimates that the introduction of personal and corporate income taxes could increase government revenue by an amount equal to 2.5% of GDP, even with reduced collection of less-efficient taxes.

Given these fiscal challenges, accessing climate and concessional financing from development partners will help Vanuatu to meet the cost of adaptation, mitigation, and disaster recovery. Vanuatu's Debt Management Strategy targets all new external borrowing to be highly concessional (i.e., with at least 35% grant component and a 10-year grace period) to keep the debt servicing affordable.[1]

The government is aiming to get the Department of Finance and Treasury to be accredited for accessing climate financing (instead of going through regional bodies), although the accreditation process can take several years (IMF 2021).

The government has also accessed contingent financing following disasters, including from the World Bank Catastrophe-Deferred Drawdown Option (Cat DDO) and ADB's contingent disaster financing (CDF) facility under the Pacific Disaster Resilience Program. After Cyclone Harold struck in April 2020, Vanuatu was able to access $10 million from the Cat DDO and $5 million from the CDF. The government also accessed CDF funds following the COVID-19 community transmission in 2022.

Aside from exploring options to mobilize resources, it is crucial to ensure that government expenditure on climate-resilient infrastructure is efficient and well targeted. Budget analysis reveals sometimes large differences between budgeted capital expenditure and actual capital expenditure (Figure 22). This is partly because of disasters, which can prompt unexpected increases in capital expenditure for reconstruction, or stall planned infrastructure projects, resulting in under-spending.

However, the volatile budget execution rates for capital expenditure also suggests the potential to strengthen public investment management. Further integration of adaptation and mitigation plans into medium-term budgeting would help identify financing gaps. It would also help to sequence large projects which can strain the bureaucracy's implementation capacity.

Finally, along with mobilizing resources and strengthening public investment management, there is a need to build fiscal buffers against climate-related shocks. The government has established an emergency fund, which can fund disaster response up to Vt300 million ($2.6 million) even before the declaration of a state of emergency. After the declaration has been made, another 1.5% of the appropriated budget for the year can be reallocated for disaster response.

Aside from maintaining the emergency fund, continuing to conservatively project HCPs revenue and using windfall receipts to rebuild fiscal buffers is another strategy to improve Vanuatu's disaster and climate resilience.

Endnote

[1] Public debt was estimated equivalent to 51.1% of GDP in 2021.

References

ADB. 2018. *Pacific Economic Monitor.* Manila (December).

Government of Vanuatu. 2019. *Vanuatu Nationally Determined Contributions (NDC) Implementation Roadmap.* Port Vila.

Government of Vanuatu. 2020. *Vanuatu Recovery Strategy 2020-2023.* Port Vila.

Government of Vanuatu. 2021. *Vanuatu's COP26 Engagement Program 2021 Final Report.* Port Vila (18 November).

Government of Vanuatu Department of Climate Change. 2022. *Declaration of Climate Emergency approved unanimously by the Parliament of Vanuatu.*

International Monetary Fund (IMF). 2021. Vanuatu 2021 Article IV Consultation. *IMF Country Report* No. 21/208. Washington, DC.

World Bank. 2021. *Dealing with Disasters: Analyzing Vanuatu's Economy and Public Finances through the Lens of Disaster Resilience.*

Figure 22: Vanuatu Budget Execution Rate

Budget execution for capital expenditure fluctuated from 185% in 2018 to 64% in 2020.

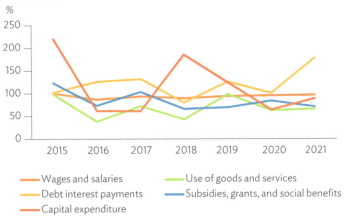

Note: Budget execution rate is the ratio of actual expenditure to the original budget.
Source: ADB estimates using data from budget documents.

POLICY BRIEFS

Financing resilience to mitigate the Pacific's climate vulnerability

The Pacific is extremely vulnerable to climate change and natural hazards, which are major challenges that hinder the development aspirations of the subregion. Of the world's top 15 nations most vulnerable to risks, five are Pacific developing member countries (DMCs) with Vanuatu, Solomon Islands, and Tonga topping the list (WorldRiskReport 2021). Many of these smaller Pacific DMCs are characterized by low-lying islands, isolated locations, small land areas separated by vast oceans, high population concentration in urban areas, and high costs of providing basic services, all of which exacerbate their vulnerability. This makes the subregion's climate financing needs large, estimated at 6.5%–9.0% of gross domestic product (GDP) annually. However, financing to date has fallen far short of needs, and access and implementation efforts have been uneven. This policy brief will highlight the vulnerability of Pacific DMCs to natural hazards, discuss current subregional efforts, and explore ways and arrangements that the Pacific could draw on to facilitate efforts in building climate change resilience and managing disaster risk reduction.

EXTENT OF VULNERABILITY

Warming temperatures and ocean acidification have led to sea-level rise, frequent tropical cyclones, drought, and extreme weather patterns, all of which impede the sustainability of economic growth in the Pacific. From December 2020 to January 2021, Fiji was pummelled by three severe tropical cyclones (Yasa, Ana, and Bina) within a short span of 6 weeks. Similarly in 2005, four cyclones (Percy, Meena, Nancy, and Olaf) struck the Cook Islands within 4 weeks (Table 1). Other destructive events have included Tropical Cyclone Pam, which struck Vanuatu and Tuvalu in 2015; and Tropical Cyclone Winston, which hit Fiji in 2016. The volcanic eruption in Tonga that occurred in mid-January 2022 is considered by scientists as the biggest atmospheric explosion in over a century. The outlook is alarming, with the recent Intergovernmental Panel on Climate Change Sixth Assessment Report pointing to more extreme conditions and increased climate variability in the future (IPCC 2021).

Other climatic impacts facing Pacific DMCs include saltwater intrusion into habitats and drinking water sources, loss of ocean biodiversity, damage to coastal ecosystems and infrastructure, decreased crop yield and food security, increased drought frequency and duration, and decreased water quality and availability. These increase the cost of delivering basic social services and hamper progress towards the achievement of the 2030 Sustainable Development Goals.

The regularity and severity of natural hazards reinforce the need for targeted and coordinated actions on climate change and disaster risk management to better understand, plan, fund, and coordinate at the local, national, regional, and international levels.

ECONOMIC, SOCIAL, AND HUMAN LOSS

The costs of recent natural hazards are beyond the Pacific governments' abilities to respond effectively using domestic resources. Between 2015 and 2020, the costs of severe cyclones that hit the subregion, particularly Fiji, Solomon Islands, Tonga, and Vanuatu, have increased and are estimated at $5.0 billion in total (Figure 1). Further, the volcanic eruption and tsunami in Tonga early this year is estimated to have resulted in economic damage equivalent to about 18.0% of GDP. The magnitude of damage and loss from past cyclones ranged from 28% of GDP from Cyclone Evan in 2012 to as much as 64% of GDP from Cyclone Pam in 2015 (Figure 2). This shows that one tropical cyclone could wipe out many years of reforms and development.

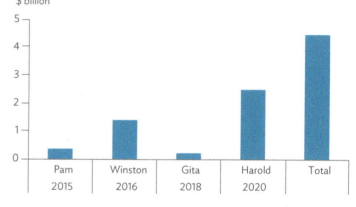

Figure 1: Economic Costs of Severe Cyclones in the Pacific

Sources: World Meteorological Organization, Secretariat of the Pacific Community.

Figure 2: Impacts of Recent Natural Hazards in the Pacific (2012–2018)

GDP = gross domestic product.
Sources: ADB estimates, and Pacific Islands Forum Secretariat. 2021. *An Overview of Climate and Disaster Risk Financing Options for Pacific Island Countries.*

Table 1: Profile of Selected Major Climate Events in the Pacific (2004–2020)

No.	Name of Cyclone	Duration	Wind Speed	Affected Areas	Estimated Damage ($ million)
1	Heta	January 2004	215 km/h	Niue, Samoa, Tonga, Wallis and Futuna	225
2	Meena	February 2005	215 km/h	Cook Islands	20
3	Nancy	February 2005	230 km/h	Cook Islands	unknown
4	Olaf	February 2005	215 km/h	Cook Islands, Samoa	10
5	Percy	February 2005	230 km/h	Cook Islands, Samoa, Tokelau	25
6	Ului	March 2010	215 km/h	Solomon Islands, Vanuatu	unknown
7	Ian	January 2014	205 km/h	Fiji, Tonga	48
8	Pam	March 2015	250 km/h	Fiji, Kiribati, New Caledonia, New Zealand, Solomon Islands, Tuvalu, Vanuatu	360
9	Winston	February 2016	280 km/h	Fiji, Niue, Tonga, Vanuatu	1,400
10	Donna	May 2017	205 km/h	New Zealand, Melanesia	10
11	Gita	February 2018	205 km/h	Fiji, Niue, Samoa, Solomon Islands, Tonga, Vanuatu, Wallis and Futuna	221
12	Harold	April 2020	230 km/h	Fiji, Solomon Islands, Tonga, Vanuatu	significant

km/h = kilometer per hour, No. = number.
Sources: World Meteorological Organization, Fiji Meteorological Service.

Apart from economic losses, there are also social and human losses. The full extent of these losses experienced from the loss of life and the indirect long-term impacts on the communities and ecosystems are enormous. The devastation caused by Tropical Cyclone Pam displaced more than 65,000 men, women, and children in Vanuatu as well as negatively impacting the livelihoods of more than 80% of the rural population; while Cyclone Harold, which struck in 2020 at the start of the coronavirus disease (COVID-19) pandemic, destroyed more than 26,000 households and affected more than 129,000 Solomon Islanders. Cyclone Harold affected 180,000 people in Fiji and caused about F$100 million in damages (SPC 2020). These losses have a ripple effect on other sectors of the economy—including agriculture, education, health, fisheries, and infrastructure—which, in turn, negatively impact the Pacific's progress toward achieving the 2030 Sustainable Development Goals.

Further, Pacific DMCs must deal with a constant state of recovery from disasters triggered by natural hazards, which has not allowed much fiscal space to plan and respond effectively to shocks. Even prior to the COVID-19 pandemic, the Pacific governments were still paying for damages caused by climatic events that occurred 5–10 years ago. The idea of climate risk insurance is also new and occasionally discussed at the regional level.

In terms of governance, the role of a robust public financial management (PFM) system is critical in accessing and managing finance for resilience. According to the Public Expenditure and Financial Accountability (PEFA) 2022 Global Report on PFM, globally, PFM systems struggle where it matters most for efficient service delivery—budget execution. The report also states that the COVID-19 pandemic has revealed that many PFM systems were not sufficiently resilient to shocks. Striking the balance between responsiveness and accountability is an ongoing challenge. Within the Pacific, the same narrative resonates as levels of progress among national systems vary. Weaknesses in areas of procurement and project management have constrained efforts of Pacific DMCs to mobilize finance at scale, directly access funding from existing and new innovative sources, and ensure that finance accessed is invested effectively.

CURRENT EFFORTS TO MITIGATE CLIMATE VULNERABILITY

Financing to build resilience is a key priority for Pacific leaders. To respond to these challenges, the Pacific is currently developing a long-term vision—the 2050 Strategy for the Blue Pacific Continent—to secure its future toward a resilient Pacific region of peace, harmony, security, social inclusion, and prosperity that ensures all Pacific peoples can lead free, healthy, and productive lives. The strategy prioritizes seven thematic areas: (i) political leadership and regionalism, (ii) resources and economic development, (iii) climate change, (iv) oceans and natural environment, (v) people-centered development, (vi) technology and connectivity, and (vii) peace and security.

Second, many Pacific DMCs, with the support of their development partners, are pursuing reforms to strengthen national institutions and PFM systems. This includes efforts to (i) have direct access to global climate funds such as the Green Climate Fund (GCF) (e.g., Cook Islands, Ministry of Finance) and the Adaptation Fund (e.g., Tuvalu, Ministry of Finance); (ii) strengthen monitoring and evaluation capabilities; (iii) ensure consistent capacity building and supplementation; and (iv) track climate and disaster risk finance flows through climate budget tagging (e.g., Fiji, Ministry of Economy). Other countries, such as Fiji, Kiribati, Palau, Samoa, Solomon Islands, and Tonga have mainstreamed climate change functions into their ministries of finance.

At the regional level, there is a Technical Working Group (TWG) on PFM and Climate Finance spearheaded by the Pacific Islands Forum Secretariat and comprising Australia, New Zealand, the Asian Development Bank, the British High Commission in Fiji, Deutsche Gesellschaft für Internationale Zusammenarbeit, the European Union, the International Monetary Fund's Pacific Financial Technical Assistance Centre, the United Nations Development Programme, and the World Bank. The TWG serves as an advisory group to the Pacific Island Forum Economic Ministers[1] Meeting on PFM and Climate Finance and operates in three areas: (i) inclusion of climate change considerations into the PEFA framework, (ii) development of a regional national implementing entity guideline for the GCF and Adaptation Fund, and (iii) development of a discussion paper on the effectiveness of climate finance in the Pacific.

In 2021, a world-first pilot of the new PEFA Climate Module was completed in Samoa to assess the responsiveness of country PFM systems to climate change. The findings suggest that, although the planning framework is robust, there is no link between the framework and the allocation of resources for climate-related activities. This hampered monitoring efforts, given the mismatch between the planning framework and resourcing. The then-chief executive officer of the Ministry of Finance of Samoa noted that the exercise has helped them to rethink how to mainstream climate change into their budget process. A paper on climate finance effectiveness in the Pacific was also developed under the TWG's oversight. The paper noted that, despite a gradual increase in climate finance flows to the Pacific, there is a disconnect between the allocation and utilization of these resources and the priorities of vulnerable people most impacted by climate change. The paper underscored the need for longer-term community resilience as a key driver.

In the past decade, the Pacific's focus has been primarily on a few vertical global funds that allocate development assistance focused on a specific issue or theme, such as the GCF and Global Environment Fund. For instance, just over $500 million has been approved by the GCF for the Pacific, $48 million from the Adaptation Fund, $459 million from the Global Environment Fund, and $120 million from the Climate Investment Funds. However, there has been little attempt at stimulating private sector engagement and private finance has been limited.

Building on efforts by the Pacific Islands Forum Secretariat and partners such as ADB, the World Bank, and bilateral partners to strengthen private sector engagement in climate finance, there is now impetus to work through the upcoming Forum Economic Ministers Meeting in August 2022 to shift attention toward mobilizing scalable and transformative private finance and tapping into new and innovative financing options. However, this will require stronger regionalism toward programmatic and multi-country interventions in key areas such as renewable energy and the blue economy. Currently, about 98% of climate finance is delivered to the Pacific on a project basis, which is not sustainable and often fragmented. Fiji is working toward launching its blue bonds to leverage private finance, building on the successful issuance of its green bonds in 2017. The Pacific Islands Forum Secretariat and partners have explored other innovative options, including a carbon emissions levy and debt-for-climate swaps.

The role of dedicated national climate, disaster, and green energy funds has also gained prominence in Fiji, Tonga, Tuvalu, and Vanuatu. Further, in Palau, the green fee charged together with departure tax for non-Palauans has benefited initiatives that support the management of protected areas in the country. The Government of Palau earned over $1 million in tax revenues in 2009 from this new green fee tax (Solomon Times 2010). At the regional level, Pacific leaders endorsed the Pacific Resilience Facility in 2019 as an ex-ante small grants financing mechanism to build resilience of communities in vulnerable Pacific DMCs.

Finally, while some Pacific DMCs pursue disaster and climatic risk insurance products, their effectiveness and coverage has been limited by expensive premiums and stringent pay-out conditions. Insurance pay-out amounts are typically too small to enable Pacific DMCs to effectively respond or recover from disasters. Support from technical assistance associated with ADB's Contingent Disaster Financing Facility has sought to fill in some of these financing gaps while initiatives such as the Pacific Catastrophe Risk Insurance Company have helped Pacific DMCs undertake reforms to address these issues.

CONCLUSION AND RECOMMENDATIONS

Pacific DMCs are among the most vulnerable in the world to natural hazards from disasters and the adverse impacts of climate change. They have successfully tapped into various sources of resilience finance with the support of their development partners. To be effective, Pacific DMCs need to be more innovative in pursuing transformative investments that could be scaled up, not just from the vertical climate and disaster funds but from the plethora of untapped opportunities from private investors, pension funds, foundations, and non-traditional partners.

Further, to ensure that current efforts are sustained and strengthened to plan, implement, monitor, and evaluate support in a timely and consistent manner, the Pacific with its development partners need to focus on the following:

(i) **Improve data collection and management.** Currently, there is no regional database that provides a single point of reference on information that could help inform targeted climate change and disaster risk management designs and initiatives, particularly the design and management of public and private investments in infrastructure and other sectors. Such information would include data on various natural hazards, classified by type, information on the types of materials used in homes that were badly destroyed, the value of the loss and damages to the Pacific, and details on available financing instruments.

(ii) **Strengthen institutional capacity for PFM and project management.** These, particularly on procurement and budget execution, are critical areas in all aspects of development, but weaknesses persist despite numerous reforms on PFM and project management support provided by development partners. There are no set ways to strengthen institutional capacity in Pacific DMCs as the level of capacity development would be determined based on the context. Noting this, the tailored regional guideline developed through the TWG on PFM and climate could be made available as resource materials to inform efforts of Pacific DMCs on PFM. Further, there are opportunities to share lessons from various infrastructure or sector-wide programs, which could be disseminated via the institutions leading this work through policy briefs, workshops, and accredited courses on specific subject matters. For instance, lessons on a climate-ready budgeting exercise and monitoring and evaluation course could be shared virtually to increase coverage and reach.

(iii) **Improve coordination on financing options.** As noted in this brief, there are financing instruments and options that the Pacific could access through development partners and the private sector. Organizations such as the Pacific Islands Forum Secretariat, through its role in the TWG on climate, could continue to support coordination and facilitate information-sharing on various financial products. Moreover, multilateral development banks like ADB and the World Bank could provide timely advice on the numerous financial products that development banks could deploy to support climate readiness and disaster risk reduction initiatives.

Lead authors: Exsley Taloiburi, Programme Adviser–Climate Finance and Resilience Team Leader, Pacific Islands Forum Secretariat; and Lily-Anne Homasi.

Endnote

[1] Consists of all 14 Pacific DMCs.

References

ADB. ADB's Work on Climate Change and Disaster Risk Management.

Aleksandrova, M. et al. 2021. *2021 WorldRiskReport*.

Atteridge, A. and N. Canales. 2017. *Climate Finance in the Pacific: An Overview of Flows to the Region's Small Islands Developing States*.

Brule, G. et al. 2021. *Technical Assistance to Samoa for the PEFA Assessment of Climate Responsive on Public Financial Management*.

Government of Fiji. Fiji Meteorological Service.

Intergovernmental Panel on Climate Change. 2021. *Sixth Assessment Report*.

Pacific Islands Forum Secretariat. 2021. *An Overview of Climate and Disaster Risk Financing Options for Pacific Island Countries*.

PEFA Secretariat. 2022. *2022 Global Report on Public Financial Management*.

Secretariat of the Pacific Community et al. 2017. *Framework for Resilient Development in the Pacific: An integrated approach to addressing climate change and disaster risk management*.

Secretariat of the Pacific Community. 2020. *Cyclone Harold Inspires New Way to Collect Data for Disaster Assessments*. 1 October.

Solomon Times. 2010. Palau Green Fee Hits the 1 Million Mark in Less Than a Year. 26 August.

United Nations Department of Economic and Social Affairs. 2030 Sustainable Development Goals.

United Nations Development Programme. 2021. *Climate Effectiveness in the Pacific: Are We on the Right Track?*

World Meteorological Organization. Tropical Cyclone Regional Bodies.

Weathering the perfect storm: ADB's climate change financing in the Pacific

Although the ongoing coronavirus disease (COVID-19) pandemic and increases in commodity prices command a lot of attention, the Pacific subregion remains highly vulnerable to the adverse impacts of climate change. Recognizing the serious implications of climate change for sustainable development, ADB is committed to mainstreaming climate change, disaster risk management, and environmental considerations into its operations, as well as scale up climate finance. This policy brief explores the broad strategies and resources that ADB is employing to help its Pacific developing member countries (DMCs) adapt to climate change and manage disaster risk.

RISING VULNERABILITY IN THE PACIFIC

Many Pacific economies are located at the intersection of the typhoon belt, where nearly one-third of the world's tropical storms form, and the Pacific Ring of Fire, a region around the rim of the Pacific Ocean characterized by active volcanoes and frequent earthquakes. The topography of Pacific economies, i.e., the fact that many are composed of small, low-lying islands spread out over wide stretches of ocean, exposes them to the adverse impacts of inundation hazards, particularly those related to weather extremes. High levels of vulnerability to weather extremes were highlighted by Tropical Cyclone Harold, which hit the Pacific in April 2020. Strong winds and heavy rainfall and floods affected about 30% of the population in Solomon Islands and 43% of the population in Vanuatu (Connell and Cruz 2020, and Cruz and Wells 2021). The cyclone severely impacted housing and public buildings, infrastructure, and crops. Reduced supply contributed to higher consumer prices and affected economies' responses to the COVID-19 pandemic (ADB 2021a).

Climate-related threats facing Pacific economies include more intense typhoons, more severe drought, extreme rainfall, increasingly frequent coastal inundation because of rising seas, and weaker marine ecosystems from bleaching and acidification. For instance, Kiribati recently declared a state of emergency as lower-than-normal rainfall increased salinity in water sources all over the country, providing a sample of what is in store for the Pacific if climate change continues unchecked. (A more detailed discussion on improving water security in Kiribati and Tuvalu is on page 18.) Kiribati is expected to experience droughts more frequently, lasting longer and with harsher impacts (RNZ 2022).

Adverse climate change impacts will affect biodiversity and terrestrial, marine, and coastal ecosystems with severe consequences for agriculture, fisheries, and tourism. By 2100, the maximum fish catch in most Pacific island economies could be more than halved compared with 1980–2000 levels (Mycoo et al. 2022). More extreme weather events cause massive damage and losses that can reach the equivalent of more than 60% of gross domestic product, as it did in Vanuatu in the wake of Cyclone Pam in 2015 (ADB 2016).

The economic disruptions and potential of even more extreme weather events associated with climate change would undermine the resilience of communities to shocks and make islands less habitable, increasing displacement and urban congestion that would have significant implications on water and food security, especially for marginalized segments of the population. Other concerns related to the adverse impacts of climate change include weaker social cohesion, learning losses, and heightened public health risks, all of which would also threaten the viability of communities.

Pacific economies are challenged to build resilience amid mounting climate change risks and coincident shocks such as the COVID-19 pandemic and international commodity price spikes. In view of limited local resources and implementation capacity, ADB provides support for climate change adaptation (CCA) and disaster risk management (DRM) in the subregion.

ADB'S POLICY FRAMEWORK FOR ADDRESSING CLIMATE CHANGE AND DISASTER RISK

Recognizing the threat posed by climate change and disasters to the long-term sustainability of development in Asia and the Pacific, Operational Priority 3 of ADB's Strategy 2030 is centered on addressing climate change, building climate and disaster resilience, and enhancing environmental sustainability. Under this strategy, ADB commits to mainstreaming climate change, disaster risk, and environmental considerations into all levels of its operations. This includes helping its DMCs access cleaner, smarter energy, transport, and urban solutions and follow a low-emission development path aligned with their respective nationally determined contributions under the Paris Agreement. ADB will also help DMCs integrate CCA and DRM into their development planning and budgeting, as well as strengthen disaster response and recovery by boosting financial preparedness and supporting measures to "build back better."

Adapting to climate change while ensuring environmental sustainability, managing disaster risk, and strengthening institutions to bolster resilience to shocks are also central to ADB's differentiated approach to supporting fragile and conflict-afflicted situations as well as small island developing states. Seven out of ADB's 14 Pacific DMCs are classified as both (ADB 2021c).

The Pacific Approach 2021–2025 builds on Strategy 2030 and maps out how ADB will help its 12 smallest Pacific DMCs realize more inclusive, resilient, and sustainable green (and blue) growth. CCA and DRM form one of the Pacific Approach's 7 priority implementation areas. Under Objective 1 (Prepare for and respond to shocks), ADB will address the underlying causes of climate vulnerability in the subregion through more comprehensive planning and response measures to accomplish the following:

- Support DMCs in analyzing potential impact from weather extremes, including sea level rise and geo-physical hazards on people, housing, and infrastructure.
- Support DMCs to use the evidence on climate change and disaster risks to undertake transformative upstream adaptation planning and to inform the design of resilient investment pipelines.
- Deliver quick-disbursing assistance in the wake of disasters.
- Provide contingent finance and insurance mechanisms.
- Enable DMCs to access international climate finance.
- Expand climate change assistance from the project level to the country and subregional levels, including support for nationally determined contributions.
- Continue to climate-proof all investments.

This will be complemented by sustained efforts to (i) strengthen economies, health systems, and public institutions against shocks; (ii) increase the coverage and quality of basic infrastructure and services, including promoting renewable energy for power generation and the sustainable financing, management, and maintenance of assets; (iii) create enabling business environments in the Pacific; and (iv) invest in high-quality social services, including education and skills training.

PUTTING POLICY INTO ACTION

Direct financing and knowledge support. By 2030, ADB aims to have at least 75% of its committed operations (on a 3-year rolling average) supporting climate change mitigation and/or adaptation, and to have climate finance from its own resources to reach a cumulative total of $100 billion for 2019–2030. In 2019–2021, ADB committed $16.8 billion to CCA and DRM (Figure 3). Investments in mitigation accounted for the bulk of the total over the 3-year period. Of the ADB total, $375.8 million was committed to the Pacific (Figure 4).

In the Pacific, ADB is scaling up its work in CCA and strategic DRM projects in climate-sensitive sectors such as transport and energy. The number of approved projects with CCA and DRM elements increased by an average of 28.6% a year, and their combined amount by 85.1% a year, in 2018–2021 (Table 2). Although approved projects declined in 2021, it must be noted that investments continued to place priority on CCA, given Pacific island economies' overall small contributions to carbon dioxide emissions.

More specifically, ADB is helping Pacific DMCs to generate geo-referenced data on sea level rise projections and the future impact of inundation hazards on urban and coastal communities as well as on infrastructure. A multi-hazard disaster risk assessment on Tonga's main island and location of its capital, Tongatapu, was completed in 2021 and more assessments are about to start in the Cook Islands and Vanuatu. Risk assessments help to (i) generate evidence on prospective impacts and costs of failing to adapt, support CCA and DRM proposal development, and access additional external climate funds; and (ii) develop upstream transformational adaptation plans as well as investment pipelines for resilient infrastructure, nature-based solutions, and resilient social and health services.

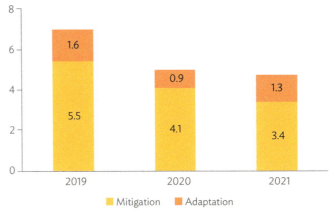

Figure 3: ADB Climate Change Financing
($ billion, based on commitments)

ADB committed a total of $16.8 billion in 2019–2021, mostly for investments in mitigation.

ADB = Asian Development Bank.
Source: ADB. Climate Change Financing at ADB (accessed 27 June 2022).

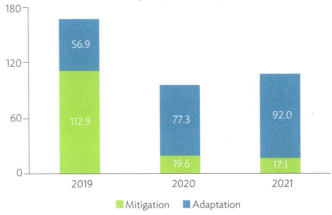

Figure 4: ADB Climate Change Financing in the Pacific
($ million, based on commitments)

ADB committed $375.8 million to the Pacific in 2019–2021, with a marked shift to financing adaptation during the period.

ADB = Asian Development Bank.
Source: ADB. Climate Change Financing at ADB (accessed 27 June 2022).

The Asian Development Fund, which provides grants to DMCs at high or moderate risk of debt distress, has financed a wide range of initiatives in the Pacific. In 2021 alone, it backed CCA finance initiatives including improvements to the efficiency and resilience of Solomon Islands' transport network and Vanuatu's power distribution system; and efforts to restore inclusive, climate-resilient economic growth in Fiji and Tonga. It also supported complementary measures such as preparatory work for planned climate-resilient infrastructure projects in eligible Pacific DMCs, public financial management reforms to help build fiscal resilience in the Marshall Islands, and enhanced social protection for vulnerable groups in Palau.

Table 2: Pacific Projects Related to Climate Change Adaptation and Disaster Risk Management, by Primary Hazard Type
(in $ million and number of approved projects)

The number and value of approved Pacific projects with CCA/DRM elements have risen substantially since ADB's Strategy 2030 was adopted in 2018.

Year	Biological		Geophysical		Hydrometeorological		Multihazard		Total	
	Amount	No.	Amount	No.	Amount	No.	Amount	No.	Amount	No.
2018	–	–	1.5	2	126.1	7	23.5	3	151.1	12
2019	–	–	–	–	90.7	4	235.9	10	326.7	14
2020	617.7	18	–	–	91.3	7	210.9	8	919.9	33
2021	134.6	6	–	–	337.0	2	57.9	3	529.5	11
Total	752.3	24	1.5	2	645.1	20	528.2	24	1,927.0	70

– = none, ADB = Asian Development Bank, CCA = climate change adaptation, DRM = disaster risk management, No. = number.
Source: Asian Development Bank estimates.

The Asian Development Fund also contributes to ADB's contingent disaster financing facilities, including the Pacific Disaster Resilience Program. This facility seeks to strengthen participating DMCs' responsiveness and resilience to natural hazards such as recurring weather extremes and health emergencies. The facility also supports the implementation of policy actions to reduce underlying disaster risk and enhance preparedness, and provides fast-disbursing, flexible contingent disaster financing for timely response, early recovery, and reconstruction that can be rapidly disbursed when a state of national disaster or emergency is declared (ADB 2017; ADB 2020a). The financing component, which covers 10 Pacific DMCs during the third phase of the program, has enabled ADB to quickly support emergency and early recovery needs in the wake of disasters and complements other risk financing tools such as governments' contingency budgets, national disaster funds, parametric disaster insurance, and traditional indemnity insurance. Achieving previously agreed DRM policy actions determines eligibility to access financing under this facility; and participating DMCs have agreed to post-program partnership frameworks based on a gap and needs analyses to further address policies, reforms, and initiatives that promote CCA and DRM.

ADB also helps develop and disseminate knowledge on climate change and disaster risk. Publications on climate change run the gamut from examinations of developmental solutions for the region to national-level risk assessments to guides on enhancing feasibility studies and design of specific types of projects. ADB is also implementing technical assistance to help develop climate-resilient investment pathways in the Pacific by (i) improving DMCs' access to climate change information for strategic decision-making; (ii) enhancing DMCs' planning and policy development processes to better adapt to a changing climate; and (iii) supporting projects and programs, with focus on upstream inputs and partnership building (ADB 2020b).

Collaboration and partnership. Besides government counterparts, much of ADB operations are implemented in cooperation with development partners as well as other national stakeholders, including civil society and private sector organizations. They play a key role in helping ADB to scale up support for CCA and DRM.

ADB administers a number of funds and facilities to finance CCA and DRM. One of these is the Ireland Trust Fund for Building Climate Change and Disaster Resilience in Small Island Developing States, established in 2019. Among other activities, this fund has supported technical assistance under the Pacific Disaster Resilience Program as well as the complementary Strengthening Social Protection in the Pacific technical assistance project, which helps Pacific DMCs respond to COVID-19 and climate- and disaster-related shocks by broadening social protection systems.

ADB also works with the Global Environment Facility, a multilateral trust fund that finances developing countries to implement their commitments under major international environmental conventions. This fund has backed the development of sustainable, climate-resilient urban water supply and sanitation systems in the Pacific, as well as climate-resilient road reconstruction in Vanuatu following the devastation from Cyclone Pam in 2015. Pacific DMCs are also benefiting from regional technical assistance initiatives to build coastal resilience through integrated, nature-based solutions, and to protect and develop natural capital.

Further, ADB was the first development bank accredited to administer finance in the region on behalf of the Green Climate Fund (GCF) (ADB 2021b). ADB's Pacific DMCs all have national designated authorities to serve as liaisons with GCF, but accredited development partners provide a channel through which DMCs, particularly those without their own accredited entities at the national level, can access funding. These partners also offer the added benefit of augmenting local capacity as needed during proposal and implementation. Through its partnership with ADB, GCF has funded projects in the Pacific to promote renewable energy, together with complementary technical assistance to bolster implementation and related policymaking, and sustainable transport and water supply systems.

CONCLUSION AND RECOMMENDATIONS

Pacific economies remain highly vulnerable to the adverse impacts of climate change and natural hazards, including weather extremes, sea level rise, and waterborne and vector-borne diseases. Limited resources and ongoing shocks and stresses make it challenging for them to strengthen resilience. In response, ADB is committed to mainstreaming CCA and mitigation into its operations and scaling up mobilization and provision of climate finance. It manages a wide range of funds and facilities to support climate finance investments, provides technical assistance and knowledge products, and is well positioned to help DMCs access international climate finance.

In the Pacific, ADB seeks to employ more comprehensive upstream planning and response approaches to help address climate-related vulnerabilities. In examining the existing interrelations between climate change and Pacific systems and practices, the barriers to long-term adaptation must be incorporated into the formulation of truly holistic and strategic responses.

Through this approach, ADB will help DMCs to access, localize, and use climate and disaster risk data to inform upstream planning, including at the national level and across sectors, and to generate a holistic framework for the planning and implementation of projects. Such planning would help facilitate actions to mitigate risk from sea level rise and extreme weather events, as well as develop policies and economic incentives conducive to resilient, green, and blue recovery.

ADB will also continue providing finance (emergency and otherwise), insurance mechanisms, and assistance to access other international sources of funding. In keeping with plans to scale up support for climate finance, ADB will continue to help its DMCs pursue vital investments in ocean health, nature-based solutions, and sustainable use and restoration of natural assets. Further, given its crosscutting nature, ADB will establish greater linkages between climate change and sectors such as education, health, social protection, and tourism.

Finally, the role played by improved governance in strengthening resilience cannot be emphasized enough. More consistent efforts to build, as well as longer-term augmentation of, government agencies' capacity (whether in CCA and DRM or other sectors) to plan for and respond to risks to long-term socioeconomic development, coordinate and manage development initiatives, and manage and maintain key physical assets should help sustain know-how as well as enhance project implementation at the country level.

Lead authors: Cara Tinio, with contributions from Alexandra Galperin, senior disaster risk management specialist, Pacific Department, ADB, and Jeffrey Bowyer, senior climate change specialist, Pacific Department, ADB.

References

ADB. *ADB's Work on Climate Change and Disaster Risk Management.*

ADB. *Projects & Tenders* (accessed 27–28 June 2022).

ADB. 2016a. *Asian Development Outlook 2016: Asia's Potential Growth.* Manila.

ADB. 2017. *Pacific Disaster Resilience Program.* Manila.

ADB. 2018. *Strategy 2030: Achieving a Prosperous, Inclusive, Resilient, and Sustainable Asia and the Pacific.* Manila.

ADB. 2020a. *Pacific Disaster Resilience Program (Phase 3).* Manila.

ADB. 2020b. *Technical Assistance for Support to Climate-Resilient Investment Pathways in the Pacific.* Manila.

ADB. 2021a. *Asian Development Outlook 2021: Financing a Green and Resilient Recovery.* Manila.

ADB. 2021b. *Pacific Approach, 2021–2025.* Manila.

ADB. 2021c. *ADB Launches Integrated Approach to Support Fragile and Conflict-Affected Situations and Small Island Developing States.* Manila (15 June).

ADB. 2021d. *ADB Raises 2019–2030 Climate Finance Ambition to $100 Billion.* Manila (13 October).

ADB. 2022. *How Ireland is Helping Climate-Proof the Pacific.* Manila (16 March).

Connell, J. and P. Cruz. 2020. Twin shocks: Dealing with COVID-19 and Tropical Cyclone Harold in Solomon Islands and Vanuatu. *Pacific Economic Monitor.* Manila: ADB (July).

Cruz, P. and N. Wells. 2021. Gearing up for recovery: COVID-19 and the private sector in Vanuatu. *Pacific Economic Monitor.* Manila: ADB (July).

Government of Australia, Department of Foreign Affairs and Trade. *Crisis Hub: Tropical Cyclone Harold.*

Government of Vanuatu. 2020. *Vanuatu Recovery Strategy 2020–2023.* Port Vila.

Green Climate Fund. National Designated Authorities.

Gutierrez, L. 2022. Building a Resilient Pacific: ADB's partnership approach toward reducing risks from shocks, delivering sustainable services, and supporting inclusive growth. Presentation for the Pacific Regional Debt Conference. Hybrid meeting. 5–8 April.

Mycoo, M. et al. 2022. Small Islands. In Intergovernmental Panel on Climate Change. *Climate Change 2022: Impacts, Adaptation, and Vulnerability.* Contribution of Working Group II to the Sixth Assessment Report of the Intergovernmental Panel on Climate Change. Cambridge, United Kingdom: Cambridge University Press.

Radio New Zealand (RNZ). 2022. Droughts on Kiribati are more frequent, last longer, and more intense says UN. 17 June.

Velasco-Rosenheim, R. 2021. ADB's new development strategy for its 12 smallest Pacific island developing member countries. *Pacific Economic Monitor.* Manila: ADB (July).

44 Economic Indicators

Nonfuel Merchandise Exports from Australia
(A$; y-o-y % change, 3-month m.a.)

( ) = negative, A$ = Australian dollar, m.a. = moving average, y-o-y = year-on-year.
Source: Australian Bureau of Statistics.

Nonfuel Merchandise Exports from New Zealand and the United States
(y-o-y % change, 3-month m.a.)

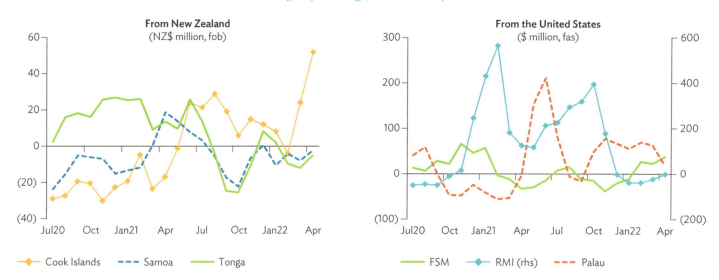

( ) = negative, fas = free alongside, fob = free on board, FSM = Federated States of Micronesia, m.a. = moving average, NZ$ = New Zealand dollar, rhs = right-hand scale, RMI = Republic of the Marshall Islands, y-o-y = year on year.
Sources: Statistics New Zealand and United States Census Bureau.

Economic Indicators 45

Diesel Exports from Singapore
(y-o-y % change, 3-month m.a.)

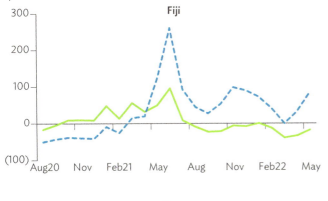
Fiji

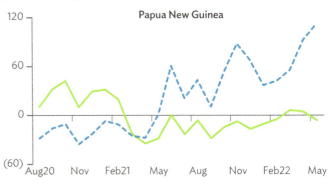
Papua New Guinea

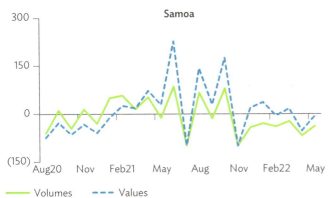
Samoa

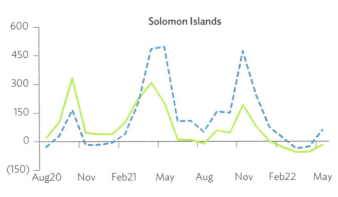
Solomon Islands

— Volumes   --- Values

( ) = negative, m.a. = moving average, y-o-y = year on year.
Source: International Enterprise Singapore.

Gasoline Exports from Singapore
(y-o-y % change, 3-month m.a.)

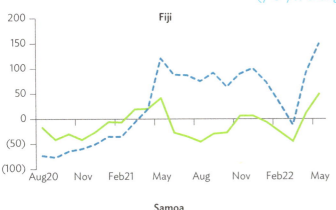
Fiji

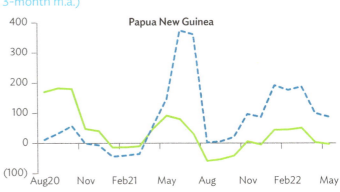
Papua New Guinea

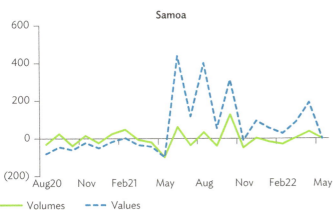
Samoa

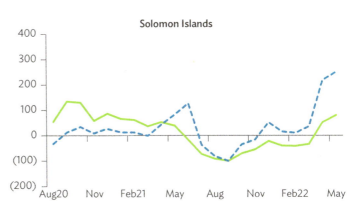
Solomon Islands

— Volumes   --- Values

( ) = negative, m.a. = moving average, y-o-y = year on year.
Source: International Enterprise Singapore.

Economic Indicators

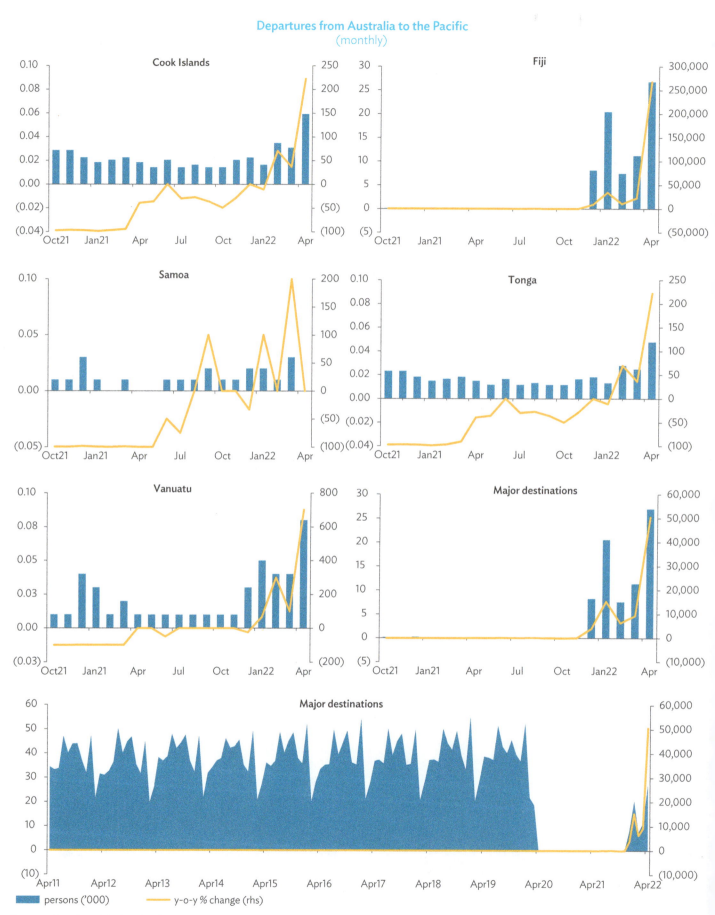

Departures from Australia to the Pacific (monthly)

( ) = negative, rhs = right-hand scale, y-o-y = year on year.
Source: Australian Bureau of Statistics.

CPSIA information can be obtained
at www.ICGtesting.com
Printed in the USA
LVHW071910111122
732929LV00009B/337